SINGLE GIRL BLISS

HOW TO STOP FEELING ALONE & START FEELING ALIVE

by Leslie Kaz

Single Girl Bliss: How to Stop Feeling Alone & Start Feeling Alive
By Leslie Kaz

For information on getting permission for reprints and excerpts, contact:
leslie@lesliekaz.com

ISBN: 978-1-7342778-0-7

- For every single woman out there. -

YOU ARE
NOT ALONE.

TABLE OF CONTENTS

INTRODUCTION

" **W**hen life hands you lemons, make lemonade." — said some annoyingly cheerful Pollyanna-type a long time ago. And since people are still saying this today, there must be some value to it. So the question is, how? How do you make lemonade out of years and years of relationship lemons? How do you mix sugar into the breakups, divorces, loneliness, and the feeling that there must be something horribly wrong with you or you'd be living the proverbial happily-ever-after already?

I decided to write this book after spending twenty-one fruitless years (pardon the pun) searching for Prince Charming and finding nothing but frogs. And all the kisses in the world were not going to change those frogs into anything resembling Mr. Right. So one day I threw in the towel and finally found happiness on my own. Ha! Actually, it was a much longer process than that. What I had to discover was that happiness was there all along, I was just failing to notice it as I distracted myself with The Endless Search amongst the sea of frogs. Oh, so many frogs.

MY SINGLENESS WAS LIKE A LITTLE GREY CLOUD THAT HUNG OVER ME EVERY WAKING MOMENT.

It's not like I consciously thought about it every minute of every day. "Hi, I'm Leslie and I'm hopelessly, pathetically ALONE!" "Hiiiii, Leeesliiieee!" But in everything I did and everywhere I went, I was reminded in some way that I was single and not like everyone else. When I was sitting in a soul-crushing meeting at work and fantasizing about standing up, giving the room a big F-U complete with finger, and waltzing out the door never to be seen again, I was reminded that I couldn't because I was alone and who else would pay the Netflix bill. When I was on a girls' weekend and being begged by my LTMFs (long-time married friends) to regale them with tales of my romantic life, I realized that I was the entertainment and not truly on their level. And at social events of all kinds, I found myself being the 3rd, 5th or any other odd number of wheel that exists.

The really sad part is that I truly wanted to be happy. I mean, who doesn't want to be happy? But my happiness was a picture I had painted in my head, with me standing next to the prince who finally succumbed to the kiss, transformed from his former frogginess, and loved me so much that it hurt. And bought me a fat rock and a big house in the hills and a Mercedes and told me I could work if I wanted to, but he already made so much money that it was my choice. Sigh.

If you picked up this book then I'm guessing that your happiness picture looks something like this or at least has in the past. Hopefully you understand that there are other pictures out there. There are selfies, for God's sake! There's the selfie of you sitting in your Mercedes parked in the driveway of your big house in the hills, wearing the fat rock that you bought with the money you made from your kick-ass new career, just because you love yourself so much it hurts!

Okay, maybe that's a wildly optimistic picture, but the point is that discovering what makes you tick as an individual and looking inside yourself for the answers instead of endlessly searching for someone else to provide them is an incredibly liberating and cathartic experience. It's about figuring out just who you are and what makes you happy RIGHT NOW, regardless of your romantic station in life. You have to do the work here, but I promise if you do you will get there. You will find your new picture of happiness where you're the star.

Now, this doesn't mean that you have to give up on the notion of ever transforming a frog into someone you want to spend eternity with. Being in a truly loving, devoted, mutually-respectful romantic relationship is one of the most amazing things in the world. What it does mean is that until that fateful frog comes hopping into your life wearing a crown, you have the obligation to make yourself happy. Right now!

If all of this seems too daunting, let's consider the alternative. You could continue to sit on the sofa on Saturday nights, eating Chunky Monkey while binge-watching old seasons of The Bachelor on DVR, all the while checking your Tinder matches. Then go to bed wondering what's wrong with you and imagining the happy life you'll have AFTER you meet Mr. Right. OR, you could find that happy life right now and be blissfully single until it changes, if you end up even wanting it to change.

This is not going to be super easy; I need to tell you that right now. You're going to have to wage war against your current mindset around being single. You're going to have to step outside your comfort zone and do things you never thought you'd do or maybe ever even wanted to do. You're going to have to figure out who you are. Who YOU really, truly are as an individual and start taking care of that person.

YOU'RE GOING TO HAVE TO STOP LOOKING OUTSIDE YOURSELF FOR THE KEYS TO HAPPINESS AND KNOW THAT YOU HAVE THEM INSIDE OF YOU RIGHT NOW.

Trust me, it can be done. It's been done by me and I have no special powers that enabled me to do so. Nor did I just wake up one day all happily single and ceremoniously dump in the trash my shoe box full of mementos of past relationships that I'd been hanging onto to prove that the frogs really did love me at some point. No, it was a process, a journey, to coin one of the latest self-development buzz-words. But it's the best damn journey I've ever taken! And you can take this journey, too, and end up on the beach with a cocktail in one hand and the spa menu in the other, while being fanned by tanned, 20-somethings who look like they stepped off the cover of a fitness magazine. Or your own blissful single girl equivalent, anyway.

Let me tell you how my personal journey began (insert harp music here)...

First, some background information. I got married when I was

18. Yes, 18. And no, I'm not from West Virginia. But after I spent my high school years with nary a date, no date to homecoming, no date to the prom, no date on a random Friday night, for God's sake, I was already well-versed in what's-wrong-with-me thinking. Then I met my ex-husband during the summer between high school and college. He actually wanted to be with me and that was like dangling a Snickers bar in front of a kid at fat camp! Since I had virtually no self-esteem at the time, I embarked on a five-year relationship with Frog #1, who was not a bad guy, just not the right one for me. We got engaged over Christmas my freshman year of college and were married the summer after, much to my parents' dismay. Injecting a healthy dose of self-worth into me may have avoided this situation, Mom and Dad, jus' sayin'. After four years of a doomed-from-the-start marriage, I divorced, and thus began my twenty-one year roller coaster ride of dating, relationships, breakups, togetherness, loneliness, ups, downs, elation and devastation.

After disastrous breakup number 87, I was lying in a crumpled heap on the floor sobbing it out over the phone to my BFF. "Well, it should be getting easier, right?" she asked. Wrong! She's clearly an LTMF. In her quest to be supportive and comforting, she had no idea just how many things were wrong with that question. After I hung up the phone, I decided that I never wanted to feel this way again. That I didn't want it to "get any easier" because the next relationship I got into would be the be-all-end-all. I was done playing games (after 21 years!) and the next person to walk into my life would be THE one!

Hearing me say this one day, a well-meaning coworker gave me a book called "Calling in 'The One'" by Katherine Woodward Thomas. I read the introduction and was hooked! Katherine was ME – similar age, similar relationship history, similar angst about it all. I felt like the book had been written just for me and I was ready to dive into it whole-heartedly. The premise of the book is that if you follow this 7-week, day-by-day plan (as the author did) of ridding yourself of the garbage in your head and readying yourself for The One to appear, appear he will!

So, I embarked on the 49-day plan with gusto, which included reading a short chapter each day and then doing an exercise. Many of the exercises were very worthwhile, if not embarrassing. On one of the days, you had to call up your BFF and tell her that by a specific date (a year from now!) you'd be married. Well, I decided I wouldn't do that, but I did call up my BFF and told her that in one year's time I would be with the person I was going to spend the rest of my life with. Yeah! That would be great!

On another day, you had to write down all of the negative thoughts you were getting rid of that were keeping you from being available to accept The One and then burn the piece of paper as a sacrifice to the relationship gods. Okay, I embellished that description a bit, but that's basically what it was, and I again enlisted my patient (and married, mind you) BFF to do this with me. Yep, I made her write down her own negative thoughts that she believed were holding her back in her life and toss them into the fireplace with me. I'm sure she thought I was completely nuts, but that's the great thing about a BFF, they have to love you anyway.

Eventually I got to day 49 of the "Calling in 'The One'" program and when I completed the exercise for that day I expected to feel different somehow, to have this renewed outlook on men, dating, relationships and The One. Instead something entirely different happened. Through completing this program I didn't so much prepare for The One to arrive as much as I realized I hadn't been treating myself well. At all. I was expecting the frogs to love me and have respect for me, when I clearly didn't love or respect myself. So, I decided that I was going forgo dating for six months and start treating myself well instead. Before that time was even up, something magical happened. I became happy, blissfully happy, on my own.

I HAD BEEN SPENDING SO MUCH TIME SEARCHING FOR SOMEONE ELSE, SOMEONE TO "BE WITH," SOMEONE TO MAKE ME NOT ALONE, THAT I FORGOT TO RECOGNIZE EVERYTHING GREAT ABOUT BEING SINGLE.

And believe me, there are A LOT of great things about being single! I've now been a blissful single girl for four years and I have no plans to change that status. I've never felt more liberated, more alive, or more badassy than I do now, and I wish the same for every other single girl out there who's ever laid in bed at night trying to fall asleep and sadly thinking, "I'm alone." So, in the end I was right. When I called up my BFF and told her that in a year's time I would be with the person that I would spend the rest of my life with, I was right. Turns out The One I was looking for was actually me.

So, if you're wracking your brain trying to figure out why in the world you're still single when everyone else is in a relationship. If you're asking yourself questions such as, "What's wrong with me?" or "Why does God hate me?" Know that this book is here to help you. It would give you a big ol' hug and a cookie if it had arms and an oven. This book is not about dating, not about relationships, other than the one you have with yourself. It's about being happy as a single person, about being happy between relationships instead of desperately searching for the next one, and it's about being happy with yourself so that if and when the next relationship comes along it's a happy and fulfilling one. This book is not about how to date better or how to reel in The One, it's about how to live your best life possible as a single person, a side effect of which might be you dating better and reeling in The One. This book is for the perpetually single, the between relationships single, the recently single, and those contemplating becoming single. It's also for the "serial relationshipers," who are tired of that ride and want to get off, but don't know how.

SINGLE GIRL BLISS IS FOR SINGLE WOMEN WHO ARE READY TO GIVE UP THE ENDLESS SEARCH AND START LIVING THEIR BEST LIVES RIGHT NOW.

Again, you don't have to give up on your dream of having a wonderful, loving, romantic relationship, but read this book and you'll learn how to live happily in the meantime, how to treat yourself like a princess, and how to be ready when and if The One shows up. And who knows, you may just end up blissfully happy on your own like I did. If life has handed you relationship lemons, I'll show you how to make single girl lemonade!

DEFINITIONS

This will help you navigate the Leslie-isms used in this book.

LTMF: Long-time married friend. Someone who has been married long enough to not remember what it's like to be single, if they ever even knew. They will say stupid things, such as "You're so cute, I can't believe you're not married already," and "I just don't know how you do it on your own." Many years of marriage has turned their brains to mush, so don't be too hard on them.

FROG: Man who, no matter how many times you kiss him, just won't be able to achieve princedom for you. Leave these men alone. They may be cute, but they're not for you.

THE ENDLESS SEARCH: The quest by a single person to find another single person with whom to mate. Mine lasted 21 years and, you guessed it, was ENDLESS! Until I ended it (take that!), which reduced it to a little pile of dust. Muahaha!

SINGLE GIRL BLISS: The most awesome state of being there ever was! (Wink!)

- Part 1 -

GETTING YOUR MIND RIGHT

CHAPTER 1

YOUR MINDSET IS EVERYTHING

Yep, single girls, we're jumping right into the mindset work. "But why?" you whine, "It's so hard!" Yes, it can be difficult to delve into the inner workings of your psyche and extricate all of the garbage that's been holding you back from being happy, but I start this book with this chapter because it's the most important. If you read no more than just this first chapter, at least I will have given you the tools you need to get your mindset right. But you won't read just this first chapter, will you, cuz the rest of the book is kick-ass, as well!

The hardest part about being single is your own thoughts surrounding it - your mindset. That's right, it's not having to haul in the groceries yourself week after week, and silently begging and pleading for someone else to please please please do it, just this once. Our thoughts make up everything about who we are. If we're sad, it's due to our thoughts. If we're happy, that's also due to our thoughts. Our thoughts about ourselves determine how we feel about ourselves. Our feelings about ourselves determine what actions we take in life and how we interact with the world. And our actions determine how our lives actually play out. But it all starts with our thoughts and that's why it's uber important to address them first. Subsequent chapters in this section will directly tackle the top ten limiting thoughts that we single girls are prone to feeling about ourselves and our singledom.

The first step to getting your mindset right as a single woman is to take stock of what you believe about yourself today. Our beliefs are made up of the thoughts that we've thought over and over again. If you've thought to yourself every day for the past twenty years, "My thighs are too fat," then by now that's not just a fleeting thought you're having, it has become a belief for you. No matter what anyone else says or what the mirror may reflect to the contrary, you believe that your thighs are too fat and that's that, dammit! Your current thoughts and beliefs are made up of everything that you've experienced up until now. If your parents told you over and over again that you were a terrible singer and they laughed when you said you wanted to join the school choir, then no matter how good you think you sound belting out "Jesse's Girl" in your car, you're not likely to do it in public unless you're super drunk at a karaoke bar in another town. The thought, "I'm a terrible singer," has become a belief for you and you don't even have to consciously think it for you to know that it's "true."

What things have you thought over and over that have turned into beliefs for you about being single? Do you believe that you're unlovable? Do you believe that there must be something fundamentally wrong with you because you're STILL single? Do you believe that people look down on you because you "can't find a man?" What makes these beliefs so dangerous, other than making you feel bad and being crappy things to think about yourself, is that you take action in your life based on these beliefs and those actions you take create your very existence!

IN OTHER WORDS, NEGATIVE BELIEFS ABOUT YOURSELF CAUSE YOU TO FEEL BAD ABOUT YOURSELF, WHICH CAUSES YOU TO TAKE FAULTY ACTION IN YOUR LIFE, WHICH IN TURN CAUSES YOU TO LEAD A LESS-THAN-HAPPY LIFE.

For example, if you believe that people look down on you because you can't find a man, how does that make you feel? Well, it makes you feel inferior to everyone else. And what does feeling inferior cause you to do? It causes you to jump into any relationship you can possibly get just so that you can start feeling normal. And where does that action get you? It gets you into a hell of a lot of relationships that should've ended after the first date! To elaborate on this, it gets you into bad relationship after bad relationship, which kills your self-esteem and your self-worth, you get treated poorly, you put up with things you know you shouldn't, you go through breakup after breakup, and what are you left with? A whole lotta nuthin'! Plus, people looking down on you because you choose losers and then put up with all of their crap. And weren't you trying to avoid people looking down on you in the first place? Do you see the vicious cycle that negative beliefs get you stuck in? Our thoughts influence everything in our lives.

Realizing that you have the power to change your thinking and thus change your beliefs about yourself is one of the most eye-opening things you'll ever learn in life. And the subsequent feelings you have about yourself and the actions you take because of those feelings can completely change your life.

DID YOU KNOW THAT YOU CAN THINK ANYTHING YOU WANT?

Let that sink in. You have the option of believing anything you want to believe, no matter what your parents taught you. No matter what society tries to influence you to believe. No matter what you have believed for most of your life. No matter what has happened to you or what you have done. This seems like a no-brainer, right? But it's almost like we need permission to change our thoughts. Especially when a negative thought is so ingrained in us that it becomes a negative belief for us. It feels like we need a crow-bar to get it out of our brains. Well, I'm here to be that crow-bar for you, single girl! I grant you permission to change your thinking and I'm going to show you how to do it.

As you get on the path to creating a blissful single life, the first step is to not only take stock of what you believe about yourself today, but also to take responsibility for it. Your life as it exists today was created by every decision you have ever made. That's right, you and only you got you here. "But," you say, "what about my older sister being so critical of everything I did growing up that I can barely decide what to have for dinner without second-guessing it a hundred times?" Okay, maybe your sister needs to be smacked upside the head for treating you that way. But you're an adult now and you can choose what you think about her, what you think about her behavior, and how you're going to let it affect you. So, if you think you're not happy, you must accept that the reason for that is you and your thinking. This is great news! What, it doesn't sound like great news? It sounds like it's all your fault? The reason this is great news is that first of all you can give yourself a gold star for all of the good in your life. Secondly, if you're feeling that you're less-than-happy, it's also you who has the power to change that.

It's easy to blame our current situation on something outside of our control. For example, it's easy to say, "I'm not happy because I'm alone." However, as soon as you start blaming circumstances, you give up your power to change your life. It's much more empowering to understand why you are where you are today, accept that you and only you got you here, and start making the necessary changes to live a happier life. It's important that you understand why you're not living the most blissful version of your life. For so many single women, the answer to that question is that you feel your real life begins once you meet your ideal mate and the two of you begin your life together. There is a reason we hang onto that thought instead of creating the life of our dreams right now and that reason is that it's been a belief for us for so long.

So, how can you create happiness for yourself just by changing your thinking? Remember that the actions we take in our lives are based on feelings that we have. Feelings are not optional. Feelings happen involuntarily as a result of the thoughts we think and beliefs we have. And our actions are a result of our feelings. So, if we change our thoughts, we create new feelings, which in turn causes us to take different actions in our lives. In other words, our thoughts lead to what we create in our lives. While this may sound scary, it's actually brilliant!

SINCE THOUGHTS ARE A CHOICE AND CAN BE CHANGED TO WHATEVER WE WANT THEM TO BE, SO CAN OUR LIVES. WOO-HOO!

A lot of times we think that the things that have happened to us in our lives or the things that are just a certain way and can't be changed (circumstances) are the things that dictate our lives. But what's really going on here are the thoughts and feelings we have about these circumstances. It's not the circumstance, it's the thoughts we have about that circumstance. Once we understand that we have the power to change our thoughts, we also realize that we have the power to change our lives. No situation can keep you from finding your bliss. This means that even if you're single for the rest of your life, you can still be as happy as humanly possible. Whew! Right?

Now, I'm not going to tell you that there are no bad situations in life, that every situation is neutral until you assign an unhappy feeling to it and make it bad. There are things that happen in life that I think we can all agree are not good. Loved ones die. Houses burn down. Hearts get broken. And right after one of these things has happened to you, you're not expected to put a positive spin on it, and be grateful that your house burned down and you lost everything because now you get to buy new stuff. You're entitled to your negative thoughts and emotions when something truly bad has happened to you. That said, it doesn't serve you to dwell on those thoughts and emotions, and carry them around with you forever. That's not the ticket to living a blissful life. Once you're past the initial shock and pain of a bad situation, then you can choose new thoughts, put that positive spin on it, and head to the mall!

So, if our thoughts control everything and all of our thoughts are choices, wouldn't it be a good idea to figure out what we're thinking on a daily basis that's causing our lives to be the way they are? It's actually the most important thing you can do on the road to finding your bliss. Remember, a thought that's repeated over and over again becomes a belief. What do you believe about yourself and your circumstance of being single that's holding you back from being happy? What do you tell yourself every day? It's pretty eye-opening to realize what we've been believing about ourselves.

In addition to taking responsibility for where you are today in your life, you must also take responsibility for letting go of the past as it pertains to your singleness. We've all heard about the importance of letting go of your past and focusing on your future, I'm sure. Pick up any self-help book and there will be a section in there devoted to not blaming your parents for the fact that you're broke and drink too much, forgiving your former friend for stealing your Jimmy Choo's, and accepting the fact that your ass will always be just a little bit too big in proportion to the rest of your body. But I'm talking about more than just forgiving Frog #3 for cheating on you with your BFF. I actually like to call it making friends with your past. "Hi, Past. Even though I feel like you've screwed me over time and time again, let's be besties so that I can start creating a happy future for myself, m'kay?" Sure, making friends with your past does involve some forgiveness and acceptance, but what if you took a different approach to dealing with your past? I'm talking about a whole new way of thinking here. What if you believed that your past happened exactly the way it was supposed to have happened? What if you believed that everything in your life has happened FOR you and not against you? How would this change things in your life? Revolutionary, huh?

If you truly believed that everything that has happened to you in your past has gotten you to where you are now, and that where you are now is getting your life on track as a single woman, then doesn't it stand to reason that you should not only accept your past, but embrace it? I know it's hard to believe that all of the terrible things Frogs have done to you in the past, all of the ways society has discriminated against you for being single, all of the self-doubt you've encountered about your ability to ever be happy on your own are good things. They weren't good, in and of themselves, but they shaped who you are today and who you are today is a strong woman. How do I know that? Because if you weren't strong, if you didn't have some mental bench pressing going on somewhere inside of you, you wouldn't have picked up this book.

A STRONG WOMAN LIKE YOU IS ABLE TO TAKE HER PAST, THE GOOD AND THE BAD, GIVE IT A GREAT BIG BEAR HUG AND THANK IT FOR SHAPING THE WAY YOU ARE TODAY.

Now, let's change the way you think about your past. You're not trying to put your past behind you. You're not trying to shove it way back into the depths of your closet behind those skin-tight Jordache jeans and brown suede Peter Pan boots, never to be seen or heard from again. You're appreciating it for what it's done for you. Here's a little thought exercise for you:

INSTEAD OF THINKING: My parents didn't love me enough so therefore I'm not lovable and that's why I can't make a relationship work.

THINK: My parents loved me as much as they were capable of, and if it wasn't enough that's not on me. I'm as lovable as it gets and I'm going to prove it by making my relationship with myself work. I'm going to love the hell outta myself!

INSTEAD OF THINKING: Frog #12 dumped me because my thighs are too fat and my thighs have always been too fat.

THINK: Frog #12 was an idiot and I'm glad he dumped me otherwise I'd still be stuck with him. My thighs are too fat only if I think they are, and if I do think they are then I have the power to do something about it on my own terms.

INSTEAD OF THINKING: My friends are all married and they've always looked down on me because I'm STILL single.

THINK: My married friends are actually well-meaning and want me to be happy. But they're also a little jealous of me because they don't have the freedom I have. I think I'll go out tonight and dance with men who are inappropriately too young for me, while my married friends stay home watching a Fast & Furious marathon on Netflix.

Please write down every thought you're thinking about your past—relationships, dating, how your parents/family/friends/society has made you feel about yourself and your singleness, and then write a counter thought that allows you to make friends with your past. This is what will get you into your new mindset of being a blissful single girl.

Now that we've talked about changing our thoughts in order to change our lives, I'm going to clue you in on a little secret that's going to take your new thoughts and rock them into your kick-ass new existence. It's God. Okay, half of you just cringed and some of you even put this book down, but pick it back up and bear with me here. I'm talking about the all-knowing force that created the earth and all of us and the trees that made the paper on which this book is printed. For some, that's God. For others it's Source or the Universe. It doesn't matter what you call it; it's the same thing. It's the energy from which everything, and I mean everything, is composed. This all-knowing force is responsible for everything that happens in every minute of every day of every year, from now until eternity. This includes everything that happens to you! And this force, which we'll call the Universe from here forward, is friendly and wants you to have everything in life that you want.

There have been many tomes written on how God/Source/Universe helps us in our lives, and you'll find some of my favorites mentioned here and there throughout this book, so I'm not going to go into great detail here about the inner workings of it. Suffice it to say that it exists and it's here to provide you with what you want, but you gotta place your order and you gotta do it right. The Universe is like a computer – you tell it what you're looking for and it will give it to you, but just like a computer you have to tell it exactly what you want in the right way, otherwise you'll find yourself in a garbage in/garbage out situation. So, how do you tell the Universe what you want? Do you fill out a little order form like you do at the sushi restaurant? I'll take two pieces of incredible wealth, two pieces of never-ending love, and four pieces of model body, with a starter of miso soup. No, you tell the Universe what you want through your thoughts. Ah-ha, she brought us back to thoughts again!

And now I'm going to bring us back to food again (yay!). If you go to a restaurant and you order a turkey club with a side of fries, you can be pretty sure that you're not going to get a pastrami on rye with a side of coleslaw. You were very specific about what you wanted and the waiter brought you just that. The Universe works in the same way and you place your order with your thoughts. So, if I'm always thinking about all of the things I don't have and all of the ways my life is lacking (called scarcity mindset), then I'm just going to get more scarcity and lack. I've placed my order with my thoughts and the Universal waiter has dutifully brought it to me. You don't order a pastrami on rye if what you want is a turkey club. Is it lunchtime yet?

If what you've been focusing on is the lack in your life – lack of love, lack of happiness, lack of a Lexus – then the Universe will give you exactly that. Now do you see why our thoughts are so important and why I needed to begin this book with the mindset chapter?

YOU'VE GOT TO GET YOUR MINDSET RIGHT BEFORE YOU CAN EXPECT ANYTHING ELSE IN YOUR LIFE TO CHANGE FOR THE BETTER.

I'm sure you've heard people talk about "putting it out there." What they're talking about is putting it out there to the Universe. Telling the Universe exactly what you want and knowing that in one way or another you'll get it. I'm going to give you a couple examples in case this is the first time you're hearing about all of this and your head is spinning.

I first heard about the Universe and its power to make things happen for us about fifteen years ago from Dr. Wayne Dyer and his book "The Power of Intention." Dr. Dyer basically says in that book that if you set your intentions (thoughts) on something and stick to them steadfastly, the Universe will provide. Great! So, I started down the merry path of setting my intention on finding the love of my life. The years went on and I read more books that touched on the Universe and its power to give. And I continued to focus my thoughts on finding the love of my life. Time wore on, Frogs came and went, and still no Love of Life 1.0. I started to think that the whole thing was BS or that maybe it worked for some people, but not for me.

What I didn't realize was that while placing my order with the Universe for the love of my life, I was also greatly focused on the fact that he hadn't shown up yet. In addition, I was following up my order with actions that weren't congruent with what I wanted. I was dating any old Frog who would have me and not saying, "Wait a minute, does this guy fill my order?" Eventually, I gave up my thoughts of scarcity and lack that surrounded the topic of love (more on this later), and wouldn't you know it the Universe finally provided. In all of this time that I was searching for love outside of myself, I was stuck in a mindset of scarcity and lack so that it wasn't possible for me to truly love myself. Once I gave up my scarcity mindset, the Universe said, "You want great love, you got it!" And what I found was the glorious love of self. That's what had really been missing. And myself and I have been living happily ever after ever since. When you have a loving relationship with yourself, you have a loving relationship with the Universe because the Universe IS you, and the Universe will love you back and do everything it can to make you happy. No matter what higher power, if any, you believe in, it all comes back to YOU. The power is within you and works through you, which is why your relationship with yourself and loving yourself are so important.

Another example of the Universe being on our side and fulfilling our wishes is this: several years ago I lost a job I'd had for eight years. I was unemployed for quite a few months with no one else to pay the bills and no job prospects on the horizon. I went into a pretty deep depression and started reading books to try to help myself out of it since I couldn't afford therapy. Ha! One of the books said to create a "vision board." You've probably heard of vision boards before, but if not it's a piece of poster board loaded with images that you cut out of magazines or print off the Internet and paste to it. Like a Pinterest board that you can touch. The images are all things you want in life, like a big house, a Mercedes, a hunky neurosurgeon husband, whatever. The idea is that by creating this board you're placing your order with the Universe for these things. You're supposed to look at it multiple times a day, and feel and know that these things will be yours. I was unemployed and depressed, so I thought what the hell I'll create a vision board, can't hurt. Besides, it'll give me something to do other than watch Judge Judy. So, I covered the dining room table with magazines, scissors, glue sticks, and wine, and came up with a vision board I was happy with. I dutifully looked at it day after day and did my best to feel like these things were already there for me and were just itching to show up.

A few months later, I landed a job and thoughts of the vision board faded away as I happily re-acclimated to normal life. I finally shoved the board in a closet when I was going to be out of town and someone was coming over to cat-sit for me. I didn't need anyone seeing my very personal vision board. A couple years passed and I was cleaning out the closet where I'd stashed the long-forgotten board. I pulled it out and looked at it. Holy crap if I hadn't gotten almost everything on there! I had pasted photos of beautifully designed homes because I wanted to start my own interior design business. I didn't even think it was possible at the time I put it on the board, but here I was an interior designer with her own business. I had also pasted photos of travel destinations and had been to all of them except one. The funny part about that was that when I pasted them on the board the photos didn't even represent specific places I wanted to go necessarily, just travel in general, and they were photos that had appealed to me and also happened to be in my magazines. I had a photo of a gondola in Venice that I had cut from an international coffee ad, which represented Italy for me. Guess where I ended up going? To Venice! And that was only because I was on a business trip to Germany and Venice was the easiest Italian city to get to by train, not because I specifically wanted to go to Venice (not that Venice isn't awesome, mind you, because it is). I almost couldn't breathe as I looked at the order I'd placed with the Universe and realized how it had been fulfilled.

Now, there are more ways to place your order with the Universe than just a vision board. There are the thoughts you think on a daily basis, the things you focus on. There are visualizations you can do where you picture yourself in the scenario of what you want and you really feel the feelings that you would have if you were already there.

There are daily affirmations that you do where you tell yourself that you already are what you desire to be. But how does all of this pertain to the unhappy single girl who's trying to find her bliss? Well, being happy as a single woman has to do with more than just coming to terms with your singleness, it has to do with living your best life. And living your best life is not possible if your thoughts are stuck in scarcity and lack.

I, myself, was so busy focusing on what I didn't have that I didn't realize what I did have. For twenty-one years!

AS DR. WAYNE DYER SO ELOQUENTLY STATED, "IF YOU CHANGE THE WAY YOU LOOK AT THINGS, THE THINGS YOU LOOK AT CHANGE."

That's exactly the type of mindset shift I'm talking about here. This is exactly what's going to get you from sad and alone to blissfully single. All I had to do was change my mindset about myself and my life, place my order with the Universe, and the world around me and everything in it changed for me. All I had to do. Right. It was a pretty tall order, of course, but I'm going to tell you how I did it.

The first thing I had to do was decide to put The Endless Search on hold. I wasn't ready to completely give up The Endless Search at this point, but I was willing to pause it until a later date to be determined. That meant that I had to take down my Match.com profile, hide all of my dating self-help books in the basement, and cancel my subscription to Modern Bride. This step sounds easy, but there are a lot of thoughts that get in the way while doing this. We're about to address some of these thoughts in the rest of Part 1. The next thing I had to do was start noticing all of the great things about being single.

AS SOON AS I MADE UP MY MIND TO FOCUS MY THOUGHTS ON WHAT WAS GOOD ABOUT BEING SINGLE, I STARTED TO REALIZE HOW MUCH THERE REALLY WAS.

I had been so focused on the scarcity and lack associated with not having found The One that I believed that most things about being single were negative. But when I shifted my mindset I shifted my outlook on life. Finally, I had to take this new outlook and use it to do good for myself.

Now, everything didn't just go happily according to plan: Leslie decided to change her thinking and so all of her thoughts just instantly changed and everything around her changed, too, and everything was sooo great and she started farting rose petals. Of course it's not that easy. Your brain doesn't want you to be blissful as a single girl. It believes that the only safe thing you can do is be part of a couple and it will do everything it can to keep you on that track. After all, that thinking has gotten you this far and you're still alive. Plus, our brains want to do the easiest thing possible in order to save us from suffering, and the easiest thing is always to not change. Your brain thinks that the easiest thing is to continue on the same path of thinking that you've been on. Why? Because it's been pounded into it since birth! By your parents, by other family, by your friends, by society. Your brain is lazy and only needs to be reprogrammed with a new, energizing mindset. Treat your nay-saying brain like your nagging mother. Roll your eyes and move forward anyway.

TO RECAP, HERE ARE THE STEPS YOU NEED TO TAKE TO CHANGE YOUR MINDSET AROUND BEING SINGLE:

1. Stop or press pause on The Endless Search
2. Focus your thoughts on what's good about being single
3. Start treating yourself and your life well

The reason we have to stop or press pause on The Endless Search is because being single is hell when you're desperately searching for someone, but can be pure bliss when you're not. You've just got to make the decision that that part of your life is done, or at least on hold for now. Step 2 is the hardest and the rest of this section goes into how to battle those thoughts that are holding you back from having a blissfully single mindset. I've already explained why our thoughts are so important to our happiness. They're everything, really. Finally, once you understand what thoughts are plaguing you and how to change them, we'll get into how to start treating yourself and your life well by figuring out who you are, what you want, and how to get it. You're on your way to bliss, you lucky single girl!

THE WORK

1. What beliefs do you have about yourself that are not serving you well? About how you look? About your talents? About what you have or don't have?

2. What things have you thought over and over that have turned into beliefs for you about being single?

3. What actions or inactions have these negative beliefs caused you to take in your life?

4. What circumstances have you blamed for the reasons that you're single?

5. What negative thoughts do you think about your past that are not serving you well in your present?

6. What do you focus on on a daily basis that places your order with the Universe for something you don't want?

7. Look at your answers to the questions above. Take each answer and rewrite it in a positive way. For example, if you said, "I believe that I can't be happy on my own," rewrite that statement to say, "I believe that I have the power within me to make my life as happy as I want it."

8. Write the following statement ten times: "I am a kick-ass single girl who has the power to create my best life and I believe that being single rocks!"

CHAPTER 2

AWFUL, UNTRUE, LIMITING THOUGHT #1: "THERE'S SOMETHING WRONG WITH ME"

If you're thinking that there's something wrong with you because you're STILL single and can't seem to find someone, how does that make you feel about yourself? Well, it probably makes you feel inadequate, weird and different from everyone else. Unattractive, stupid, boring, too tall, too short, too fat, too thin, perpetually having spinach in your teeth, the list goes on and on.

There probably actually is something wrong with you, but define "wrong." There's something wrong with your happily married neighbor, too, and SHE found someone. The truth is, there's something "wrong" with all of us! And believing that there's something wrong with you is not the reason you're single. It could be the reason you're not happy, however. It could be creating negative feelings within yourself that not only led you to date the wrong people in the past or not put yourself out there to begin with, but are also keeping you from having the happiest life you could possibly have right now.

One of the most difficult things we all have to deal with in life is rejection. We've all been rejected by someone at some point in our lives. Romantic rejection seems to top the charts, though, when it comes to bringing about feelings that there's something wrong with us. For example, if you read the introduction then you know that I didn't date in high school. And it wasn't for lack of wanting on my part. I wanted nothing more than to be picked up by some boy in his dad's car, taken to a movie and dinner at Chili's, and then awkwardly kissed and groped before being deposited back at home by curfew. The boys just weren't interested in me. What was wrong with me? I was outgoing, smart, funny, energetic, had a lot of friends, and was involved in things like sports and student council projects. I was also 5'9" tall, with a sturdy, Eastern-European frame and about 15-20 extra pounds, which in high school might as well be 1,000 extra pounds. And while not unattractive, my face probably wasn't going to win any pageants. In other words, I wasn't the cute, little girl that every guy wanted to date. But did that mean there was something wrong with me?

Well, I guess I could've laid off the McDonald's, but otherwise no, there was nothing wrong with me. Is there something wrong with being tall? Is there something wrong with not having a body that looks like it's going to crumble under the weight of your backpack? Is there something wrong with not having a model-perfect face? There wasn't anything wrong with me, there was only what was wrong with my perception of myself (my thoughts) and how my feelings surrounding those thoughts made me interact with those around me. Did I put myself out there like I actually wanted to date? Or did I make buddies out of all the guys so that I wasn't setting myself up for rejection? I don't think those poor, adolescent-insecure boys ever even saw me as a dating possibility because I never really saw myself as one, either. Oh, there were probably a few with secret crushes, but they were too insecure to ever act upon them. Hence, I entered the adult dating world thinking that there was something wrong with me and I'm quite certain I carried that thought all the way through my dating life.

THE REASON I STRUGGLED SO MUCH WITH BEING SINGLE WAS THAT I DIDN'T HAVE THE CONFIDENCE FOR IT.

Single was something that I just *was* most of the time, by default, but I couldn't *be* it. Because I believed that if someone was interested in me or wanted to be with me then there wasn't anything wrong with me after all and I was okay. Consequently, if there didn't happen to be anyone interested in me or wanting to be with me at any given time then there was something wrong with me. Imagine going through most of your adult life thinking that there was something wrong with you and hard core jonesing for the only thing that would make you okay – a relationship. Or maybe this is/was you? The only thing worse was when someone had me and then decided that they could most definitely live without me. It didn't even occur to me until six months after being unceremoniously kicked to the curb that there was actually something wrong with them and the only thing wrong with me was my choice in Frogs.

The most detrimental thing about thinking that there's something wrong with you because you're single, other than being completely untrue, is that it causes you to have negative feelings about yourself that then cause you to act in ways that don't get you what you want. In order to get what you want in life (happiness, fulfillment, ass-kickery), you have to believe that you're worthy of it, first and foremost. For example, if you think that you must be unlovable since you're still single, then not only do you think you're unlovable to men, but you probably also think you're unlovable to your friends, your family, the lady who does your toes, the checker at the grocery store, the whole damn world! If this is true then you feel unworthy as a human being. And if you feel unworthy as a human being, is the Universe there to help and support you? Do you celebrate your singleness in all its glory? Do you run out there and try new things and meet new people and have a blast while doing it all? No, you probably sit at home watching Netflix with the cats. (Side note – there's actually nothing wrong with sitting at home watching Netflix with the cats. Trust me here.) But these feelings of unworthiness caused by the thought that you're unlovable have caused you to live a lesser life than you know you want and are capable of.

Believe me, it takes some serious work to change the thought that there's something wrong with you when you've thought that way your entire life, or at least since high school. It doesn't happen overnight. The worst thing you can do is actually try to pinpoint the thing that's wrong so that you can fix it. I used to spend countless hours wracking my brain trying to figure out why in the world I was still single when *everyone else* was in a relationship. Sometimes I could look at it logically and realize that there really was nothing wrong with me or at least nothing any worse than anyone else. This would make me feel better until the subsequent thought entered my mind of, "Okay, so then when is it my turn?" If there was really nothing wrong with me then when was it my turn to find someone?

I saw everyone else around me coupling up and there I sat, all by myself. I started equating it to the game Musical Chairs.

There was me, walking around a circle of loveseats instead of chairs, with several other women. There was a man sitting on one side of each of the loveseats and when the music stopped we were supposed to sit down in the nearest one. Sitting next to us would be our soon-to-be mate. The music would stop and I'd scramble to the nearest loveseat, but some size-2 biatch would throw an elbow and make it there a second sooner. So I'd look for the next closest one, and of course find that every loveseat was now occupied with a happy couple and I was the only one left standing. As per usual. The worst was when I was playing this game with the same ladies that I had played the last round with. They had all found loveseats, the relationships contained within obviously not working out, and now they were back in the ring to take another swing. And then they would find loveseats again, while I, of course, remained standing.

I actually remember a time when an example of Dating Musical Chairs played out right before my very eyes. I'd broken up with someone I thought I was going to marry and I was alone. Again. Not long afterward a friend of mine met someone. They got married, were married for a while, got divorced, and she met someone new (who she ended up marrying) all in the same time it took me to not meet anyone at all and continue to be alone. WTF? Did the Universe hate me and not want me to be happy? Actually, the Universe loved me and was trying to save me from a life of doom with any of the Frogs I had been with. See, the problem with wondering when it's going to be your turn is that just like "there's something wrong with me," it's a limiting thought. It's a belief that there's something lacking in your life because you don't have someone, and it's an order placed with the Universe for more of the same.

So, how do we single girls stop believing that there's something wrong with us, wondering when it's going to be our turn, and get happy and live our most blissful lives possible? Drumroll please... Just stop. Stop thinking that. There's nothing wrong with you just because you're on your own. The only thing wrong with you is that you think there is something wrong with you and you dwell on it all the time, causing the Universe to agree with you. I know some incredibly fabulous women who are STILL single and there's nothing inherently wrong with them.

IN FACT, MAYBE THERE'S SOMETHING REALLY RIGHT WITH YOU, DID YOU EVER THINK OF THAT?

Maybe there's something really right with dodging the bullets from all those failed relationships. Maybe there's something really right with not picking up the dirty socks off the floor while your partner swills beer on the couch in his underwear. Maybe there's something really right about not getting a dutch oven in bed first thing in the morning. Google it. Maybe there's something really right with not having the relationship your best friend has. I mean, is it really all that great? I bet she gets dutch ovens on a regular basis.

This will take some time and repetition to really sink in, but replace that thought of "there's something wrong with me" with something that looks like this:

I'm awesome (cuz ya knows ya are)! And because I'm awesome I feel great about my life and everything I do. And because I feel great about my life and everything I do, I'm going to sign up for that rock climbing class. And because I sign up for that rock climbing class I become a kick-ass rock climber who qualifies for the Olympic team now that it's an event. And because I'm now an Olympic badass, love and adoration are showered upon me by many, most importantly myself!

And as for, "when is it my turn?" It's your turn right now! It's your turn to live your best life right now and to attract all of the wonderful things into your life that you want. Show the Universe how awesome you are with your thoughts and actions, and the Universe will help a sista out.

THE WORK:

1. What things have you believed are "wrong" with you that you've blamed as the reason you're single?

2. How can you rewrite those beliefs to mean something different? For example, if you said, "I believe that I'm single because I'm strong and men are afraid of me," can you say instead, "My strength is one of my greatest assets and has gotten me far in life. Anyone who can't handle my strength is not someone I want to be with anyway?"

3. Now write down everything that you believe is really right with you!

4. Write the following statement ten times: "I'm single because I'm being given the opportunity to create an amazing life for myself with nothing holding me back!"

CHAPTER 3

AWFUL, UNTRUE, LIMITING THOUGHT #2: "I'M NOT WHOLE ON MY OWN"

Your perception of yourself as not whole if you're not in a relationship is just that, a perception. It's not real. It's those bloody thoughts again that can spoil everything. It's those thoughts that make you feel insecure as a single girl and cause you to renew your subscription to Match.com even though all you've been matched with in the past two years are men who are 45 years old and live in their parents' basement because they're "between jobs." It's your duty to yourself as a single girl to stop looking for something outside of yourself to make you whole and start looking inside instead. The emptiness you feel inside may need to be filled by something other than a romantic relationship.

Looking outside of yourself for something that you perceive to be missing within yourself is a dangerous game to play. First of all, you can't expect someone else to make up for your perceived shortcomings. Why would someone else even want to take on that responsibility? It's like expecting someone else to pay off your debt. I'm pretty sure if you polled all of the single people in the world and asked them what qualities they're looking for in a mate, "up to their eyeballs in debt and needing a li'l help" wouldn't be one of them. A lot of what attracts us to someone are the qualities about them that we perceive to not possess ourselves. You need to work on developing those qualities within yourself.

Secondly, when you do place that responsibility on someone else then you're also handing them the power over your own happiness. I hate to break it to ya, but only you can make you happy. No, you argue, I'm most happy when I'm in a relationship with someone great and he brings me flowers and he compliments my hair and he tells me he doesn't care how fat I get, he'll love me anyway. HE makes me happy! Au contraire, it's your thoughts about what he's doing that make you happy. It's your thoughts about yourself and how those thoughts make you feel, not about him. "He's doing and saying these wonderful things to me, so I must be okay after all." You are the one who has the power to think that you're okay regardless of what anyone else is doing for you or saying to you. You can buy yourself flowers, admire your own hair, and love your own size-14 ass!

Third, you're basically saying that you can never be happy unless someone else is filling in all of your voids. Even if you're in a relationship, how often does that happen? How often does someone else so perfectly compliment you that's it's difficult to tell where they end and you begin? I don't care how happy you are with someone, they can't and shouldn't be expected to "make you whole." Single people often say that they feel like something's missing. Something is missing, but it's not another person. It's you. It's the wholeness of you and the beautiful relationship with yourself that you don't have.

THE QUEST FOR WHOLENESS, THEN, MUST COME FROM WITHIN.

Identify those things you perceive you don't have and are expecting a mate to "fill in." First, ask yourself whether you really don't possess those qualities. Be honest. If there are some areas in which you're lacking, that's fine, not everyone is going to possess absolutely every fabulousness that's out there. But are they something you can work on improving? I once had a boyfriend, Frog #30, who had a very patient temperament. I tended to be on the opposite end of that spectrum, though I'm proud to say I've done a lot of work in that area, ahem. I was always amazed at his ability to keep his cool while driving. If some bonehead cut him off, he just backed off and seemed to not think a thing of it. I would actually stare intently at his face to see if there was any expression of I'm-going-to-kill-that-guy at all, and there wasn't. Me, Road Rage Queen, would've gotten in the other lane, sped up in front of the guy, and cut him off within an inch of his bumper just to see how HE liked it! I like to think I've matured since then and have adopted more of the I'll-just-back-off-calmly attitude, not that there isn't a middle finger waving around wildly inside my car from time to time. The point is, at the time, he was the patient one and I was the type A. Now I've adopted some of those patient qualities and I don't need someone else to be the voice of reason anymore. Even when I get off track and lose my patience, I'm aware that I'm doing it and I have the power to reel myself back in if I want to.

So, if you feel that you're not good at something, say money for example, and you need someone to keep you on track, don't look to a Frog to do this for you. You're a smart girl. Hire a financial planner, or read a book or take a class on money management. If you feel that you're not up on technology — you're always the last one to sign up for the latest social media platform and your phone is so out of date that they don't even send you updates for it anymore, find a friend who's tech savvy and do what she does. Ask her to advise you on products and software, and let you know the latest stuff when it comes out.

If you're feeling like you're nobody until somebody loves you, you might be right. But who's to say that the somebody in question has to be a romantic partner? Do your parents love you? Your sister? Your BFF? Your dog?

CERTAINLY SOMEONE OUT THERE LOVES YOU, PROBABLY PLENTY OF SOMEONES, AND WE OFTEN OVERLOOK THESE RELATIONSHIPS BECAUSE THEY'RE NOT ROMANTIC IN NATURE.

A few days ago I met a couple of friends for happy hour. One of them is a LTMF, but the other is in her mid-50's and has never been married. Single Girl starts talking about all the things she's been up to lately. Her job has been busy, she's been traveling for both business and pleasure, she's been playing golf, running 5Ks, she started doing a barre class, and she was recently recruited to take on a high-level volunteer management position with a charitable organization with which she's involved. Wow, that's a busy, productive life that includes a lot of people in it. Later in the conversation, LTMF was telling Single Girl that she thought she was going to meet someone soon. Single Girl said, "It would be nice to have someone to do things with." Are you kidding me?! How many more things do you need to do, for one thing, and are you not already blessed to have plenty of people in your life with whom you do these things? Then they looked at me for my reaction and I said, "Not me. I'd rather do things with you guys." And the beautiful part was, I totally meant it.

It's easy to think you're not whole when you don't have that one other person who's totally yours and no one else's, but if you really look at your life I think you'll find plenty of people. Women tend to have lots of relationships in their lives. We have peeps we can talk to about things. If you're struggling with hot flashes, who do you talk to? Your mom. If you're struggling with mom issues, who do you talk to? Your sister. And if you're struggling with where to dump your last boyfriend's body, who do you talk to? That one can only be dealt with by your BFF, but the point is you have someone there for you. There's a statistic out there somewhere that pertains to the rapid rate in which men enter a new relationship after getting out of their previous one. Well yeah, they're men, so they don't have anyone to talk to unless they have women in their lives. In the movie Jerry McGuire, when Tom Cruise says to Renee Zellweger, "You complete me," he was probably right, but my guess is that she had the power to be complete all on her own. So do you.

The most important relationship that we tend to overlook when we need someone is the one we have with ourselves. This is the most important relationship you'll ever have, period. You know that old expression of you're born alone and you die alone? Well, it's kinda true, except that you're not really alone because you have yourself.

THE SOONER YOU MAKE FRIENDS WITH YOU, ACCEPT YOU FOR WHO YOU ARE, AND FALL IN LOVE WITH YOURSELF, THE HAPPIER AND MORE CONTENT YOU'LL BE.

People want so desperately to be loved by someone else that they forget to love themselves. If someone else loves me then that means I'm okay. But you'll never truly be okay with yourself if you don't love you. This goes for everyone, not just us single girls, but we're in the unique position of being able to focus on ourselves and find that love that's been missing. The whole second section of this book deals with feelin' the love, so if you're not there yet, don't worry, you will be.

THE WORK

1. What are the ways you've felt that you're not whole? What have you felt is missing inside of you?

2. What have you expected past partners to make up for that you considered a lack within yourself?

3. What do you expect someone else to do for you to make you happy?

4. Do you now see that you're whole on your own and you can make yourself happy? Write down new thoughts that celebrate your wholeness and not scarcity or lack.

5. Write the following statement ten times: "I am whole all on my own and I love myself because of all the ass-kickery I have within me!"

CHAPTER 4

AWFUL, UNTRUE, LIMITING THOUGHT #3:
"I NEEEEED A RELATIONSHIP/I CAN'T BE ALONE"

One year I decided that I was going to spend Thanksgiving by myself. All day, all by myself. As in, I'm not going to leave the house or interact in person with another living soul all day. I had never done this before and I wasn't sure what to expect, but it was the trial of a new experience in my Single Girl Bliss-ful life. So, I politely turned down all of the well-meaning invitations to dinner and made solo plans for the day.

I got up and watched the parade, while making and eating those cinnamon rolls that come in a tube and always scare the crap out of me when I open them. I swear I have only three fears in life – snakes, spiders, and opening a tube of cinnamon rolls. After the parade was over, I changed the channel to football and got some game-day snacks ready for myself. After that I went for a nice walk down to the lake (okay, I guess I did actually leave the house) and when I got back I started preparing Thanksgiving dinner for myself. I made a turkey breast, mashed potatoes, gravy, green beans, cranberry sauce, rolls, and pumpkin cookies for dessert. Of course,

I did eat all of this on the couch in front of the TV while wearing sweatpants, but that's one of the beauties of having Thanksgiving all on your own. I ended the day with a favorite chick flick and went to bed happy. I mean, doesn't that sound like a kick-ass day? Food, fun, and sweatpants, for God's sake!

A few days later I was talking to a friend who asked me what I had done for Thanksgiving. I told her and she said, "Oh, I could never do that." Now, this particular friend is a LTMF and my guess is that she's never spent even one day alone, much less a major holiday, so I kind of got where she was coming from. But later I was thinking about the conversation and I thought, "Really? You could NEVER do that? What exactly would happen to you if you did? Would you wither and die of sadness in a matter of hours? Would you spontaneously combust due to the stress of it all? Or would the cinnamon roll tube explode in your face, causing massive damage and requiring the need for reconstructive surgery?" (that last one could happen, BTW). It's like someone saying to you that you can never have chocolate ever again for the rest of your life. And you're saying no way, I could never do that. But really you could, right? If the Universe said that the next piece of chocolate you eat you'll die, you could find other things to take the place of that chocolate, right? Crème brûlée, key lime pie, caramels; there are plenty of things that would satisfy you and take the place of that thing you thought you couldn't live without. And after a while you might not even miss the chocolate anymore or you might find other things that you like just the same or even more.

So many of us think that we can't possibly be alone and therefore we need a relationship. We need that one person who's required to be there for us on Thanksgiving no matter what. But how many women have been left alone at a time when they really needed someone? How many husbands have died of massive heart attacks at 65, leaving their wives to spend their golden years alone? How many fathers have walked out the door on their wives and children, never to be seen again and no child support check forthcoming? These women became alone through no fault of their own and they figured it out. They figured out how to get through life and some of them probably did a great job of it. Do you think these women whined, "I can't be alone!"? Please! Sure, maybe they eventually found another relationship to be in, but for a time they had to make the alone thing work and they did it without dying. You can, too.

It's not wrong to want a relationship, it's wrong to expect that relationship to make you happy and to accept being miserable until that relationship comes along. Isn't that an awful lot of responsibility to heap on someone you haven't even met? Some of you think that if the right guy would just come along then everything would be great. Okay, how so? First of all, you're expecting something outside of yourself to make your life great and only you can do that. Secondly, you're expecting a man to manage your emotions. A man. I'm going to leave it at that. Third, even if the "right guy" came along what makes you think it would be so great? Because all of your other relationships were so great? Okay, so let's say this is Mr. Right and he's leagues better than anyone else you've ever dated. You're still going to have to compromise in order to exist harmoniously with him. Let me say that again. You're still going to have to compromise. Because you have to compromise in order to be in any relationship, romantic or otherwise. That's what interpersonal relationships are about. Sometimes and in some relationships the compromises are worth it, but I see a lot of women making a lot of huge compromises and still not being happy when they could be creating a wonderful life for themselves with very little compromise.

REMEMBER, THE RELATIONSHIP YOU HAVE WITH YOURSELF IS THE MOST IMPORTANT ONE YOU'LL EVER HAVE.

Why not spend the energy you put into miserably longing for a mate into living your best life instead? If you agree with this premise, but still can't picture yourself being alone long-term, imagine this scenario:

After being dumped by yet another Frog, our Single Girl heroine finds herself alone and terrified that she's never going to meet anyone again. Instead of focusing on what she doesn't have in her life, she decides to do some of the things she's been putting off. She quits her soul-crushing admin job and starts her own portrait photography business. With the extra freedom in her schedule, she takes up tennis and meets some amazing women friends at the club. In addition, her active tennis lifestyle causes her to lose 30 lbs and get in the best shape of her life. Her business takes off because she's so passionate about it and she's able to buy the house she's always wanted for herself. She realizes she has everything she's ever wanted – her own successful business, a house she loves, lots of friends to do things with, a hot body, and more confidence than she's ever had in her life. She loves the new her! The Frogs start sniffing around, but instead of jumping at the chance to be with the first douchebag who will have her, she has the courage to be choosy. She repels the Frogs one by one until the day one of her tennis besties introduces her to a Frog she describes as a total catch. He's smart, kind, funny, attractive, and has some cheddah. He's impressed with her story about how she started her own biz from scratch and bought her own home, and he loves her confidence and passion. This Frog is truly her prince and they live happily ever after. Now, do you think any of this would've happened if she'd just gone out with whatever d-bag came after the last one because she thought she neeeeded a relationship?

Thinking that you must have a relationship and you can't possibly be alone means a lifetime spent jumping from relationship to relationship with anyone who will have you because you just can't bear to be alone. Is this the way to live your life? It's the way to kill your self-esteem and get you into a bunch of crappy relationships, that's for sure. Part of the reason you don't want to be alone is because you see being alone as being back in The Endless Search instead of what it can be, which is the most blissful time in your life. You're better than The Endless Search. You can go to the grocery store by yourself, you can watch The Bachelor with your BFF, and you can take your best guy friend to the company Christmas party. And if it goes deeper than that and you think that if you're not in a relationship you won't have anyone to lean on or anyone to love you, then you haven't been paying attention. Family, friends, children, coworkers; these people all love you and are there for you to lean on. If they weren't, then there's no way I would've gotten this far in life, as these people were most of the time the only ones there for me.

CHANGING YOUR THINKING ABOUT WHAT YOU TRULY WANT/NEED AND WHO CAN HELP YOU GET IT, INCLUDING YOURSELF, IS THE KEY TO HAVING ENOUGH CONFIDENCE TO BE HAPPY ON YOUR OWN.

It's the key to being able to choose a relationship if you want one and not just take whatever's available so that you won't be alone. It's the key to Single Girl Bliss!

I would be remiss if I got through this chapter on not neeeeeding a relationship without mentioning the S-word. Sex. I believe that most women, and even a lot of men, prefer to have sex with someone with whom they're in a relationship. So, in this case, in order to have sex you would need a relationship. But there are several ways to scratch that itch without having to commit to someone who's not right for you. The easiest way is to take care of it on your own. Most of us have been doing this for a while so I won't get into the gory details, but you know what I'm talking about. If all you're looking for is physical pleasure or release, then this should do it for you. If you're looking for a physical connection to another human being, however, then BOB (battery operated boyfriend) is not going to cut it. You still don't need to commit to someone to have that connection, however. If a woman wants to have sex, she can find plenty of willing accomplices. There are whole "dating" sites devoted to just this. But if one-nighters with handsome strangers don't turn your crank or you're afraid you might end up with Ted Bundy, you're not alone. This is why a lot of women have that "friend with benefits." He's someone you know, like, and can trust. In this case, you are in a relationship with this person, just not the traditional definition.

If nothing but having sex with someone whom you love and are in a committed relationship with will do for you, though, then you need a relationship, right? Is sex a reason to settle for someone who's not right for you, though? Of course not. As far as I know, no one ever died from not having sex. Nuns and monks abstain from it their whole lives. For the most part, though, regular people can't be expected to go through life not having sex. It's considered a basic human need. Which is why I refer you back to one of the options I just discussed. Think of it this way, how much sex do you think people in committed relationships are really having? Especially after many years of being together? Once a week? Once a month? You'd be surprised how little it really is. Certainly you and BOB can hold out for a while, right?

One phenomenon that's present for all people is our ability to remember past good times as being better than they actually were while at the same time remembering past bad times as being not as bad as they actually were. I suppose this serves us well most of the time, as we tend not to remember pain as acutely as it was when we first experienced it and that's something we all need for survival. If women could acutely remember the pain of childbirth, the human race would die out. However, this selective memory phenomenon takes place when we're remembering past relationships, as well. We remember the good times way too fondly and the bad times as not really that bad at all. This is dangerous. This is what makes us think that any relationship is better than no relationship because even the bad stuff wasn't so bad, right, and the good stuff was oh-so-good? This is what makes us think that we can only be happy while in a relationship and therefore we can't be alone. This is not the truth. It's just a coping mechanism that our brains employ in order to survive and not crumble into a pile of rubble every time something bad happens to us. In order to be happily single, you've got to put past relationships behind you. It's okay to think about the good stuff fondly, but in a grateful-for-that-experience kind of way, not a gotta-get-it-back kind of way. Cuz getting it back exactly the way it was will most definitely not live up to your memories of it.

So often women define themselves by the relationship they're in. I once had a recently divorced friend who met a man and started dating him. He played golf and enjoyed scuba diving, neither of which she had ever done, but after a very long marriage she was ready to try new things. She went through the scuba certification classes, bought all of the gear, and started going on dive trips with this man. She also took golf lessons, bought a set of clubs, and they started playing golf together. She delighted in her newfound interests and she and this man went happily golfing and diving along for several years until it was time for the relationship to end. "Don't worry," I told her, "you can come golfing and diving with me!" But she had no interest in doing either of those things with me or anyone else. A golfer and diver was who she was WITH THIS MAN, not who she truly was. We lost touch shortly after that, but I'm guessing her new hobbies include whatever her current Frog likes to do.

The problem with this story is that she didn't have her own identity. She didn't know who SHE was or what SHE liked to do. She just went along with whatever the men in her life wanted and used her relationships to define her. There's no way to love yourself when you don't even know who you are. Talk about needing a relationship and not being able to be alone! This woman was lost. How can you be at peace on your own when you don't choose to define who that person is? Here's a different story for you:

I once had a friend who decided to try new things on her own and so she took up scuba diving. She went through the scuba certification classes, bought all of the gear, and went on a dive trip with some friends. While on this trip she met a man who was an avid scuba diver. He declared himself her dive buddy, helped her with her diving and even carried her gear for her. He made her first dive experience so great that they began dating and went happily diving along until it was time for the relationship to end. She was worried, as she found herself with no one to go on dive trips with, but she went to her local dive shop and found a group trip to go on. She knew no one on this trip, not even her roommate, and it was a little scary. But she instantly bonded with her roommate, who was a woman close to her age, and made several other friends on this trip who are still close friends of hers today. She has gone happily diving along on her own, and it has opened up so many friendships and good times that she can't imagine what her life would've been like if she'd abandoned the sport when her relationship abandoned her. Wanna guess who this woman is? (Hint – it's me!)

The moral of this story is that yes, you can be alone. You don't neeeeed a relationship. And you can't expect another person to make you happy.

YOU HAVE TO CREATE YOUR OWN HAPPINESS AND HAPPY LIFE FOR YOURSELF.

So, if you have to do that anyway, regardless of your relationship status, then what's the point of a relationship? Well, it's to have someone to share your happy life with, BUT, this also means that you can (and must) create a happy life for yourself on your own. You can find things and people and experiences, and when you have all that are you truly alone?

Just in case you're still not sold on being happy on your own, I want you to google the following question, "Are single women happier than married women?" I did this recently and was amazed at what popped up. I expected there to be conflicting viewpoints. I even expected there to be more evidence that married women are happier since that's been the convention for as long as I can remember. What I found instead was article after article citing research results that indicate that single woman are not only happier than their married counterparts, but are healthier and live longer, especially if they also have no children. Wow! Put that in your I-neeeeed-a-relationship pipe and smoke it!

THE WORK

1. What things do you believe you could never do alone?

2. Do you know women right now who do/have done any or all of these things alone? Write down their names next to each activity. If they can do it, it stands to reason that you can, too, right?

3. What other people in your life can help you with the things that you don't feel you can do on your own?

4. What compromises have you made in past relationships that have not served you well? Do you see that when you're on your own you don't have to make these same compromises?

5. In what ways have you let another person or the relationship itself define who you are?

6. How would you like to define yourself as a strong, independent single woman instead?

7. Write the following statement ten times: "I am a strong, independent, blissful single girl who can have it all and can get it all for herself!"

CHAPTER 5

AWFUL, UNTRUE, LIMITING THOUGHT #4
"I NEED TO BE TAKEN CARE OF"

L adies, this is not the 1950's. You are not June Cleaver vacuuming the living room in a dress, heels and pearls, just waiting for your man to come home so that your life can be complete. Maybe back then women needed to be taken care of by men, although World War II and Rosie the Riveter kind of shot that theory all to hell. Even so, after the war things pretty much went back to the way they were for another fifteen years or so. But nowadays women can do anything for themselves that a man can do for them, except for a few heavy lifting-type situations for which you'll need a burly friend or neighbor.

Do you need a man's paycheck or are you rockin' the career thing all on your own? If you're not making what you'd like to and you think it would be so much easier to just have a man take care of that part, well sure, it would be so much easier, but is that your reality right now? Do you truly NEED a man to provide you with more money? Is there absolutely no way you could make that money for yourself? Or is it just that you haven't considered the ways, hoping ight-with-Fat-Paycheck will come strolling into your the produce aisle? If money is your issue, and believe me I now whereof I preach, there are ways to get it that don't involve The Endless Search. Or prostitution. For one thing, you're likely not making the same amount as your male counterparts, so the first thing you should do is ask for a raise at work.

My personal story around "I need a man for financial support" thinking arose when I decided to change careers. I was drowning in a 20-year career full of drab-grey cubicles, mind-numbing work and soul-crushing meetings, working for companies who claimed to care about their employees. Thankfully I knew what I wanted to do instead and I went back to night school to get another degree in interior design. My dream was to start my own residential interior design business. And all I needed was a husband to support me while I did it. When I graduated with my degree, I still had no husband, had gotten laid off from my job, and instead of listening to what the Universe was trying to tell me, I got another soul-crushing job just like my last one. But one thing was different. When I started that job I said to myself, "I'm only going to be here 2-5 years and then I'm starting my design business." Sure enough, less than three years later I was out on my own with my new business. I used the time that I was at that company to save up a little cushion, and as fate would have it, there was a round of layoffs right when I was planning my exit strategy. So, not only did I have the money I'd saved, but I also made it out of there with a nice severance package to boot. I'm not going to say that those first few years weren't a struggle financially, the anxiety about it all almost did me in, but then it got easier and led to bigger and better things, and I didn't need a husband to support me after all, just the Universe.

There are other ways that women believe we need to be taken care of by men, as well. Home maintenance, technology, and anything to do with a car, to name a few. Are you completely helpless at home repairs or are you capable of changing a light bulb? Do you really know only enough about your computer to turn it on and get to Gmail? Can you really not change a tire? I have three words for you – Home Advisor, Geek Squad, AAA (okay, five words). I'll admit that I'm a bit of a technophobe and when I was starting my design business a few years ago, I was dating a man who was very good with computers. He helped me buy a new computer and printer, and helped me buy my first tablet. He set it all up for me, networked it all together, made it cook me dinner. After we broke up we decided to remain friends and he continued to help me with my computer stuff. But the friends thing really wasn't working for me (does it ever?) and I knew I needed to end it. I had no idea how I was possibly going to take care of my technical stuff. I literally hung onto this relationship that was hurting me just for the free tech support. Finally I ended it and I haven't needed tech support since. And when I do, there's good ol' Geek Squad.

Just because you have a man in your life is no guarantee that you'll actually get the help you need with the things you believe you can't do for yourself anyway. I was having a phone conversation with a friend of mine the other day. She's a fitness freak who is always outside walking, running, hiking or biking. Her husband is a computer nerd who is always inside googling, programming, networking or gaming. He has basically tricked out their entire house with the latest in electronic gadgetry. But they were having a problem with their pool pump (first world problems). She had tried to fix it herself and had finally called a pool guy. She actually had to get off the phone with me because he was at the door. Knowing that she's kind of a traditional girl and doesn't really like to deal with these kinds of things herself, I asked, "Why isn't Brian handling this?" She answered in a bit of an exasperated tone, "Because it's outside."

Single girls, we do not need to be taken care of at all. We can make our own money, we can change our own light bulbs and tires, and we can hire our own pool guys. The women's liberation movement came about for a reason – women knew they could do anything a man could do and we've proven it time and time again. So, put your June Cleaver heels and pearls back in the closet until a party invitation comes around, and if you need help with something, call a girlfriend.

THE WORK

1. In what ways have you believed that you need someone to take care of you?

2. Can you see a way to take care of yourself in these respects, or enlist the help of a friend or family member?

3. Write the following statement ten times: "I am perfectly capable of taking care of myself and I have a world full of people there for me when I decide I need a li'l help!"

CHAPTER 6

AWFUL, UNTRUE, LIMITING THOUGHT #5: "I DON'T HAVE ANYONE TO LEAN ON"

This limiting thought is in line with the last one, but instead of being about not having our physical needs taken care of, it's more about not having our emotional needs met. Pop quiz! Men are known for a) being able to build stuff, b) having freakishly good upper body strength, c) knowing how to wire a lamp, d) their ability to be emotionally comforting and nurturing, or e) a-c above. You get what I'm getting at here. Men are good at a lot of things and some of them are more in tune to the emotional needs of their partners than others, but let's face it, most people didn't run to Dad when someone hurt their feelings, they ran to Mom.

When people say that God is a woman, I always think you've got to be kidding me! With all of the things that women have to put up with. With all the ways that women have been trod upon and persecuted throughout the ages. With all of the ways that women are discriminated against even in our progressive American society today, you've got to be kidding me. I have one word for you – childbirth. There's no way in hell a female God would put women through this! But I'm actually not here to debate the gender of God, if that's even a thing. I'm here to tell you that when you're seeking solace from the weight of the world being on your shoulders and you're feeling that nothing can comfort you the way having a man's big, strong arms around you can, take comfort in the other women around you instead.

You have lots of people to lean on if you just look around you and none of them require you to be in a romantic relationship. Your mom, your sister, your friends, your great aunt Edna. I don't care who it is, the chances of them being able to really comfort you is at least as good as the chance of your boyfriend doing so. I actually have a few really good male friends. They're men I've known for many years and consider to be "good guys." They help me fix my car, paint my house, lift anything over 50 lbs, and generally do those things with a smile. In addition to the manual labor, they're just plain good company. I'm very grateful for these men friends of mine, but let me have a fraught-with-emotion problem to discuss and they're outta there faster than if their girlfriend just told them she was pregnant. In general, men don't like to talk about emotional stuff and it's partly because they know they have very little to offer in the way of comfort other than a hug, some pats on the back, and a there-there.

When you want real emotional comfort and someone to really lean on, your best bet is one of your besties. In fact, I know women in long-term committed relationships who are happy with their partners and will still turn to their girlfriends in times of emotional need. Other women have been where you are, they've let themselves experience the emotions, and they're not afraid to empathize with you or give you advice. Women want to comfort and nurture one another. This probably goes back to caveman times when the men were out on a hunt, and the women were left at home to pick berries and care for the children. There wasn't much to do while gathered around the evening fire other than whine about how Durg never helps out around the cave and always leaves his loincloths on the floor. Women have been comforting each other and offering advice to one another since the dawn of time.

THE WORK

1. In what ways have you expected men to take care of your emotional needs? Have they done an adequate job?

2. Make a list of all the women in your life who can and will be there for you when you need someone to lean on.

3. Write the following statement ten times: "I know there will be times in my life when I'll need someone to lean on. I have a vast network of women just waiting to help me through these times!"

CHAPTER 7

AWFUL, UNTRUE, LIMITING THOUGHT #6: "BEING ALONE MEANS BEING LONELY"

W e define "alone" as not being in a relationship. But just because you're not in a relationship doesn't mean you're lonely. It's virtually impossible to be lonely in this day and age. We are so connected in so many ways that people actually have to make specific plans in order to be truly alone. I recently took a weekend trip to a friend's cabin with her and another friend of ours. The cabin was pretty remote and she warned us before we left that there would be no cell service, no WiFi, not even a TV (What? No Netflix?!). I must admit it was a little unnerving to be completely disconnected like that. Eventually we unearthed a radio and were able to tune in an '80's station. We spent the entire weekend just hanging out, talking, laughing, and belting out "Love is a Battlefield" at the top of our lungs. The best part was we didn't feel the need to look at our phones every two minutes. The real, human-to-human connection we felt was absolutely amazing and we continue to talk about it every time we see each other!

But because I was with two friends, I wasn't really alone, was I? This is true, but the connection I made with those two ladies is the same connection I make with myself that allows me to live alone, be alone, and never feel lonely. Lonely is a mindset.

YOU'RE ONLY LONELY IF YOU ALLOW YOURSELF TO BE LONELY.

I've lived alone – no husband, no live-in bf, no roommates, no children – for nearly 25 years. There have been times during that 25 years that I've felt alone and lonely and there have been times when I haven't. The situation has remained the same – I live alone. So how can I feel lonely one minute and not lonely the next? It all has to do with my mindset and how I view not only my living situation but my life in general.

When I first moved to "the big city," I was 23 years old, going through a divorce, didn't know anyone, and had never lived alone. In fact, I had never really been alone, period. I went from my parents' home, to the dorms in college, to an apartment with my bf, to a bigger apartment when he became my husband, back to my parents' home after I left said husband, and now here I was in a new city, in an apartment of my own, knowing no one, and not even having a job. But I did have a cat. She had no idea just how valuable she was to me. She was my surrogate spouse, child and friend all wrapped up in a furry orange package whose hairballs I cleaned up off the carpet.

I absolutely hated living alone and after only a couple weeks of it I started making plans to move back in with my parents once my lease was up in a year. Then I thought maybe I could find a roommate and we'd get a two-bedroom together. Then I thought maybe I'd meet someone, we'd get married, and he and I would live together. I imagined every possible scenario to not have to live alone anymore. After a few weeks in my new city I found a job and started making acquaintances, if not friends. At least I had people to talk to while at work. But what about the weekends? Every other weekend I loaded up my laundry and my cat, and made the hour-long drive to my parents' house in a neighboring city. I can remember being truly sad to leave on Sunday evenings, and trying to figure out just how early I'd have to get up on Monday mornings to make the drive home, drop off the cat and get to work on time.

Thankfully, as time wore on and my company hired more people, I began to make friends. I stopped making the trek to my parents' house on the weekends and started to get used to living alone. A year later I bought my first home, a townhouse, and enjoyed decorating it the way I wanted. But the bigger enjoyment was of the accomplishment of being a single woman and buying a home for myself at the age of 24. I was so proud of that townhouse that was mine all mine, that I got over my dread of living alone and actually started to enjoy it.

Indeed there are many things to enjoy about living alone. But what about just being alone? What about when you're facing a weekend with no date, no plans, just you and the cat staring at each other until you go insane? How do you possibly get through it without feeling like a big fat lonely loser? This is where the mindset work comes in. First of all, are you truly alone? Physically, yes, but what about mentally and emotionally. Can you not pick up your cell phone and quickly be in a conversation with your mom about the weather? Can you not get on Facebook and find out what several people you don't know commented on someone else you don't know's post? Can you not text any number of people to find out what they thought about someone you don't know's Facebook post? Of course you can do all of these things and you can literally spend hours doing them, feeling connected and not lonely, if not a bit ridiculous.

Then there are all of the things that you enjoy doing that don't require someone else in order to be enjoyed. In fact, a lot of them require someone else to NOT be there, such as reading. I personally like to watch vapid teenager shows on Netflix and I don't need an audience while I do it. Nor do I need an audience while I eat an entire bowl of whipped cream just because I can. Avoiding the shower, forgetting to do your hair or put on makeup, and singing disco songs from the '70's to your cat while dancing around your living room, are all things I recommend you do when you have a glorious weekend to yourself. Do you see how quickly facing a lonely weekend on your own can turn into something you actually look forward to with no loneliness in sight? You have no idea how many exasperated married women out there are envying you right now. Embrace your alone time, single girl! And get a cat.

The goal of the single girl seeking bliss, then, should be to stop feeling alone and start feeling alive. If you think you're alone and lonely then that's exactly what you're going to be. Remember, the Universe delivers to us whatever we focus on.

SO, IF YOU THINK YOU'RE SO AMAZINGLY LUCKY TO BE ABLE TO CREATE THE EXACT LIFE THAT YOU WANT THEN THAT'S WHAT YOU'RE GOING TO GET!

We single girls are in such a wonderfully unique situation. We can think whatever we want, we can believe whatever we want, we can do whatever we want, and we can get whatever results we want. All we have to do is decide what it is that we want, focus our thoughts on those things, believe that we can have those things, take action to get those things, and we will have them. Of course, this is over-simplified. It takes work to even figure out what it is that we want. Then to figure out what thoughts, beliefs and actions we need to have to propel us toward those things. That's what the second part of this book is all about, so stick with me and we'll get you there. For now, just remember this. When you've crafted the life of your dreams you can never be lonely, even if you're alone.

THE WORK

1. In which situations do you feel lonely? When you're home alone with nothing to do? When you're at the grocery store shopping for just yourself?

2. What can you tell yourself about these situations that will make them less lonely? Can you find the good things in these situations about experiencing them alone?

3. Not feeling lonely anymore is not going to happen overnight. What can you do to bridge the gap between feeling lonely and being able to do anything on your own? Can you do certain activities with friends? Can you find a group to do things with?

4. What can you change about a situation to make it less lonely? (Hint: your thoughts!)

5. Write the following statement ten times: "Just because I'm alone doesn't mean I'm lonely. I enjoy my own company because let's face it, I'm awesome!"

CHAPTER 8

AWFUL, UNTRUE, LIMITING THOUGHT #7:
"LIFE IS MEANT TO BE SHARED WITH A PARTNER"

Most of us grow up thinking some version of the same thing about relationships. You grow up, you get married, you have kids, and you live happily ever after. This is drilled into us from birth and we don't really see it as a conscious choice, it just IS. As we enter puberty we start playing out this scenario with the people we date, imagining what it would be like to marry acne-riddled band geek Scooter and have his multiple babies. I actually recently unearthed a "memories" book that was a type of journal I had written as a senior in high school. There were pages for your first relationship, the person you looked up to the most, and your plans for the future. On my plans for the future page I had written that I wanted to become an interior designer, marry an architect, and have six children – five boys and then a girl. Ah, to be young and stupid again. I no more wanted to push six children out of my hoo-ha than I wanted to be covered in honey and rolled in a pile of fire ants, and yet there it was in black and white. What was I thinking when I wrote that? That's the point, I wasn't thinking.

We grow up just knowing that we're supposed to meet someone someday, fall in love, get married, and procreate. We know it in the same way that we know we're supposed to eat our vegetables, pay our taxes, and always wear matching bra and underwear. It's not an option, it just is. So, imagine how difficult it is to think any other way or consider any other option when we're raised to believe that this one thing is what we're supposed to do. But this is where we need to take a good, hard look at where these messages came from and why. Certainly everything we've grown to accept and believe is being challenged these days, so why not the notion that life is meant to be shared with a partner and there's something wrong with you if you're single?

It's a tough one to get past, as are most things that we're taught from birth, but that doesn't mean it's either right or insurmountable. The people who likely instilled this vision in us were our parents and as with everything they did for us, they believed they were looking out for our happiness. As progressive as our society has become, kids today still believe that growing up and getting married, or at least spending their lives with someone, is the thing to do. My nephew is now in his 20's, but as he was growing up I was in and out of several relationships. His other aunts and uncles on my sister-in-law's side were all married and dutifully cranking out their 2.3 children. I was the oddball and something about me being single and childless never sat right with my nephew. On one occasion he decided he was going to help me out. He was about eight years old at the time and I was in my early thirties. I was sitting on the couch and he climbed on top of me, puckered his lips and headed toward my face. "What are you doing?!" I asked as I fended him off. He matter-of-factly stated, "Aunt Les, if you're going to get married someday you're going to have to learn how to kiss a boy." The room erupted with laughter. Apparently, my singleness could be attributed to me not knowing how to properly kiss a boy. If only it had been that easy.

Not long ago I had another experience where it became blatantly obvious that children are still picking up on the notion that it's not normal to be a grownup and be alone. I was out in front of my house weeding my flower beds one day when the little neighbor boys wandered over. They were about ages four and six. "Do you live here all by yourself?" the older boy asked. "Yep, I sure do," I replied. "So, you're not married?" "Nope, not married." "Do you like living here all by yourself?" What're you, my mother? This kid was six years old! I replied, "There's your mom. Why don't you boys run along now." What I wanted to say was something like, "I may live alone, but at least that means I don't spend my days getting grilled by a six-year old on the virtues of being single vs. married!"

Bucking the system can be very hard when you've got parents, siblings, nieces and nephews, all manner of other family, friends, coworkers, neighbor children, TV commercials, the checker at the supermarket, all echoing the same sentiment. "When are you going to meet someone and get married? We just want you to be happy." And there's the rub! It's instilled in us that we must be married/attached in order to be happy. Imagine spending your entire life believing this and then trying to be happy as a single person. This is where the mindset part comes in.

YOU'VE GOT TO STOP BELIEVING THAT THE ONLY WAY TO BE HAPPY IS BY HAVING A ROMANTIC RELATIONSHIP.

So, how do you do this? Well, first of all, let's look at the truth. You've likely been in at least one relationship at this point and if you're reading this book then you're also likely not still in said relationship. Was that relationship happy? Sure, probably, at first. It might've even been great and you thought you'd found what everyone was talking about. But if it ended then it must've become not great at some point. Maybe when he stopped bringing you flowers, started farting on the couch, or slept with your best friend. So, did relationship = happiness in this case? No. What about your sister or your BFF or your coworker? Are they in relationships? If so, do they spend their time floating on a cloud while extolling the virtues of their betrothed and how ecstatically happy they are? Or do they spend the entire happy hour complaining about how he never wants to go out anymore and their lovemaking has turned into something they do between the news and Colbert? So, does relationship = happiness in this case, either? Again, no. Or at least not all the time. Now for fact number three. Have there been times in your life when you were 100% single and had an absolute blast? What about that girls trip to San Fran where you mooned people from the Golden Gate Bridge? Or the time you hiked up that steep trail by yourself, thinking you were never going to reach the top, and crying with joy when you finally did? Or what about that time you spent an entire 3-day weekend binging every episode of Sex and the City from beginning to end, while eating nothing but pizza and ice cream? These scenarios describe pure bliss and you didn't need a relationship to experience them. What we need to succeed as happy single women is more of that bliss every single day.

Here's another truth. 50% of marriages end in divorce. I don't know where "they" get this statistic, but it's been the same for as long as I can remember. But that means that 50% stay together, right? Okay, so of the 50% who stay together, how many of those do you think are happy? Let's say 50% again. This may seem like a small number, but we all know lots of couples who are less than happy, and stay together for various reasons, such as kids or not wanting to be alone. And those are just the ones we know about. There could be plenty of other couples who are not so happy, but are putting on a good face for the world. Using this math, that means 25% of couples who marry actually stay together and are happy. 75% of couples who married were either so unhappy that they actually got divorced or were unhappy but stayed in that unhappy situation. So, there's a 75% chance that if you get married it'll be bad or at least less-than-good. And this is the thing we're all clamoring for? Why would we do this? It's like buying a Powerball ticket with a one in a bazillion chance of winning. We just know we're going to beat the odds, right? And we do it because it's psychologically and sociologically ingrained in us. If I told you to give me all your money and I would invest it for you, but there was a 50% chance you'd lose it all, another 25% chance you'd lose half of it, and only a 25% chance that you'd actually make some money, would you be willing to make that investment? Very likely not. But these are the odds we follow blindly when we set about on our quest for happily ever after.

Why is this so ingrained in us, then, this need to find someone and spend the rest of our lives with that person? Back in caveman times, men needed women to keep the hearth, cook the meals, birth and mind the children, and provide bedtime follies. Women needed men to bring home the bacon (literally) and defend their way of life. We didn't just want each other, we *needed* each other. We needed each other for basic survival and propagation of the species, and so the quest to find a mate is part of our DNA. Everyone assumed their respective roles and I'm guessing it actually worked pretty well. It was the way things were until some decided the grass was greener on the other side and chose to break the mold.

NOWADAYS, WOMEN ARE BRINGING HOME THEIR OWN BACON AND DEFENDING THEIR OWN WAY OF LIFE, IN ADDITION TO EVERYTHING THEY'VE ALWAYS DONE AROUND THE HOUSE, TOO.

Which I'm guessing is the source of a large part of the discontent. "If I can do all that traditional male stuff myself, then why am I putting up with his shit?" Once we take a step back from our instincts and look at things logically, we realize that not only can we do just fine on our own now, but in a lot of cases we have the ability to do it even more happily than being tied down.

A lot of women think that settling is better than being alone. I've actually heard women say, "Yeah, he (insert bad behavior here – drinks too much, gambles away all our money, doesn't really care about his kids), but it's better than being alone." I'm always flabbergasted when I hear statements like this. How can that possibly be better than being alone when you have all the power in the world to have a happy life while you're alone? I hope any woman who has ever uttered these words or similar ones is reading this book right now. Guuurl, we gotta work on your self-esteem! Because if you can get yourself to the point where it's *not* better to be in a less-than-happy relationship than it is to be alone, then you'll never settle again. When you're a 10 in your own head, you don't want to settle for a 5 or 6, and even better, you don't need to. You can hold out, and be happy and whole on your own until an equal 10 comes along, if that's what you want.

Now, to all you single girls who are reading this book and thinking that you HAVE TO find someone because you want kids and a family, or you want help with the kids you already have, that's a whole different ball of wax. I'm still not suggesting that you settle for someone who's less than what you want just so that you can have kids with him or provide a father figure for your existing children. But I do understand that children change up the game a bit. The only thing harder than being single is being a single parent. I honestly don't know how single parents do it. There are plenty of them out there doing it, though, and doing it well. So it can be done. You can have and raise kids perfectly well on your own. If this doesn't sound like what you've been dreaming of, however, that's understandable. You still owe it to yourself to create a happy life for yourself and your children (if you already have them) while you're on your own. It will set you up to attract the type of father you want for your kids. And who knows, while you're on your journey to happiness you might find that you don't truly need that person after all.

I'm not saying that there aren't wonderful, amazing advantages to being in a relationship. Of course there are. If you've ever been in a relationship, and I'm sure we've all been in a few, then you know exactly how great they can be. There are certain things about them that can never be achieved on your own. But there are plenty of things that you have to give up, as well. It's the whole grass-is-greener cliché. Sure, being in a relationship can be amazing, but you have to sacrifice some things in order to get that. Sure, being single can be amazing, but you have to sacrifice some things in order to get that, too. In any relationship I've ever been in, I've felt like a comfortable sedan. When I'm by myself I feel like a race car. Is there anything wrong with comfortable sedans? No, I drive one right now. But is that your dream car?

How many times have I heard a married friend say that she'd love to do something, but there's no point because her husband will never do it. For example, after I started scuba diving on a regular basis, I went to happy hour with a married friend because she wanted to hear all about my recent dive trip. I told her about the turtles I saw and the eels, and about the cuteness of the boat captain's butt. She sighed and said, "I wish I could learn to scuba dive, but there's no point because Marcus will never do it." Okay, how many things are wrong with this statement? She can't learn to scuba dive on her own and go on trips by herself? She's going to let her husband dictate the experiences that she has in her own life? Yes, that's exactly what I'm saying. She's decided that she's not going to have this life experience that she'd like to have because her husband won't do it with her. That's the choice that a lot of married women make for the sake of the marriage. Is this a bad thing? Not necessarily, but it's certainly limiting.

WHAT I KNOW FOR SURE IS THAT WHEN YOU'RE ON YOUR OWN, YOU CAN MAKE ANYTHING YOU WANT OF YOUR LIFE.

If you want to get a dog, you can get a dog. If you want to eat popcorn for dinner, you can eat popcorn for dinner. And if you want to move to Korea, your rickshaw awaits. You don't have to worry about what someone else wants or what they want you to do. You just do you. Now, is this better than being in a knock-your-socks off relationship with the most wonderful man who ever walked the earth? Probably not. But it's pretty damn liberating, isn't it, knowing that you can create exactly the life that you want? And you don't need permission to do it, either.

I can't tell you how many happily married women I know who say that if something happens to their husbands they won't marry again. I always assumed this was because they'd found the love of their life already and didn't see it happening again. Either that or because they'd already experienced true love they didn't feel like they had to do it again. Or maybe because no one else would ever measure up so why bother. But when pressed further they all said that it's not because they don't believe they'll ever find love again, it's because they don't want the experience of being married again. They'd rather be on their own. Is being married that bad, I ask. No, it's just that they've had the experience of being part of a whole and now they'd like to experience being whole on their own. They want to experience what you have the power to have for yourself right now!

THE WORK

1. What ideas did you grow up with surrounding marriage or at least "finding someone?" Was getting married what you were supposed to do and you never really questioned it?

2. Have you believed that being married or coupled up is what's normal and being single is abnormal? What other societal norms can you think of that don't really serve you?

3. List the times in your life when you've been 100% not in a relationship and you've had the time of your life, even if it was with other people and not entirely on your own. Is it possible to create more of this in your life?

4. In what ways have you "settled" in past relationships? Did this settling make you feel good about yourself? Can you now envision a life where you don't have to settle? What does that life look like?

5. Write the following statement ten times: "My best life is 100% defined by me. No matter what society, my parents, siblings, or friends have told me for years and years, I get to decide what's normal for me!"

CHAPTER 9

AWFUL, UNTRUE, LIMITING THOUGHT #8: "SOCIETY IS NOT SET UP FOR THE SINGLE PERSON"

While this thought is indeed awful and limiting, it's not entirely untrue. Go to the grocery store and you will see. It's almost impossible to buy food for one person. Things are generally packaged for four people, or at least for two. I can't tell you how much food I've thrown out on a weekly basis because I just can't eat an entire loaf of bread before it goes moldy. I don't have this problem with a package of cookies, however. In any case, single people do sometimes have to try to work around the way things are in order to peacefully coexist. However, a lot of the things we think are working against us really aren't. It's our perception of the truth that's the problem.

It seems that everything around us points to being in a relationship, having a partner, walking down the street hand-in-hand. It's because everything around us points to the ideal, not the real. Even people who are in relationships look at all of the media out there and know that its portrayal of couples is idealized. I recently emailed a single friend of mine to whine about a TV commercial. In the commercial, it's Christmastime and the wife has purchased matching watches for herself and her husband. She's surprising him with them in their large, fashionable home. The husband then brings her outside to show her the surprise that he got them – matching brand new cars. They're standing in their huge, landscaped driveway in front of their multi-million dollar home. And they're all of thirty years old. Pu-lease! My friend agreed that it was total fantasyland and I felt vindicated. A few days later I was at a married friend's house. She and her husband had asked me to help them pick out the finishes for their new bathroom and the contractor was there, as well. The TV was on and up popped that very same commercial. The contractor (married) started laying into the commercial, as well. "What husband can afford to do that for his wife? And these people are younger than me!" A few more comments were made and everyone laughed at the ludicrousness of the commercial. So, you see, we single people think that everything is out to get us, to prove how great married life is and how pathetic our own lives are, but all of those idealized images make married people feel just as bad as they do us. Cuz they ain't real!

This proves that it's all in our thinking and can easily be changed. If you think of yourself as the third wheel or fifth wheel or whatever, then you will be. But if you think of yourself as spending a wonderful evening with two great friends, who just happen to be married to one other, then that's what you'll have.

THE WAY WE FEEL ABOUT OUR SINGLENESS HAS LESS TO DO WITH REALITY AND MORE TO DO WITH OUR PERCEPTION OF REALITY.

I used to think that I couldn't go to a restaurant alone. People see someone sitting alone and just assume they're sad and lonely, right? In actuality there are a hundred reasons a person could be eating alone at a restaurant. Maybe they're traveling on business and don't know anyone in the town they're in. Maybe they're catching a quick bite between appointments. Or maybe they're just tired of mundane conversation and want to focus on the enjoyment of eating instead. Because of my thoughts I felt that everyone would be looking at the single person and thinking, "Jeez, what a loser. She couldn't even scare up someone to have dinner with?" Get real! People are so self-absorbed that they're paying attention only to their own tablemates. Or more likely, their phones. You could be on fire and they probably wouldn't notice you. Once I realized that no one was paying attention to me, I started eating out by myself all the time. All I had to do was change my perception of reality (my thinking) and reality changed into something that I didn't feel was working against me.

As if having the grocery store, TV commercials and restaurants all plotting against your singleness weren't enough, sometimes you actually feel discriminated against for being on your own. I'm reminded of a story my BFF told me once. Her family was planning a vacation together and they were batting around ideas about what to do and where to go. It was her mom and dad, sister and brother-in-law, and little ol' single her. They landed on the idea of taking a cruise to Alaska. Now, as most of you probably know, cruise ship cabins are designed for two people. Sure, one person can stay in a two-person cabin, but they're going to pay the same amount as two people (and three people cannot stay in a two-person cabin). Those things are barely big enough for the two people for whom they're designed. So, here BFF's family was, getting all excited about going on a cruise, until they looked at the accommodations. Let's see, one cabin for her parents, one cabin for her sis and bro-in-law, and then her mom actually said out loud, "Oh, what are we going to do about Sherri?" Something actually has to be "done about you" if you're single.

I've experienced vacation discrimination as a single person, as well. As you know by now, I am a scuba diver and I go on group trips by myself. These trips are set up as a package, so you get your airfare, hotel room, meals, diving, transportation, etc with your trip fee. But again, the fee pertains to double occupancy in the rooms. Sure, you can have a room to yourself, but it's going to cost you this many hundreds more on top of the multiple thousands you're already paying for the trip. I've gotten around this by either finding a friend to room with or requesting a roommate if no one I know can go on the trip. I've actually made some great friends this way, so I've pretty much told discrimination to suck it, but obviously it hasn't gone unnoticed.

Aside from all of the ways society seems to gang up on the singles of the world, what probably gets to us the most are the attitudes about our singleness from the people we know well – our family, friends, coworkers. "When are you going to settle down and get married already?" "I just can't understand why someone like you is still single." "Don't worry, someone will come along someday and then you'll be happy." We've heard them all. And these sentiments are from people who are supposed to love us.

WE'RE SO PROGRAMMED TO THINK, TO BELIEVE, THAT A RELATIONSHIP IS WHAT WE WANT, WHAT WE SHOULD WANT, WHAT WE NEED, WHAT WILL MAKE US WHOLE, THAT WE FEEL INADEQUATE IF WE DON'T HAVE ONE.

It's getting past that feeling that sets you free. It's changing your thinking about your singleness that will allow you to hear these statements and laugh them off instead of going home and eating a pint of Chunky Monkey.

Here's a little mind twist for you. What if all of those people who look down on you or pity you for being single are actually doing it for a reason that's not even about you? What if their contempt or sympathy actually stems from a little bit of jealousy? Or maybe a lot bit of jealousy! We haven't really talked specifically about all the good things there are about being single yet, that's later in the book, but once you realize these things, you see what coupled-up people see about you that you don't currently see. When we single women look at couples, we see all the good things about being in a relationship and we feel bad about what we don't have. Don't you think couples do the same thing? The grass is always greener, right? Your married friends are looking at your singleness and seeing all the good things about it that they don't have!

I actually had a couple of LTMFs be really honest with me about this one evening several years ago. We were on a girls golf weekend trip in the mountains and we went to a bar one night. A tall, young, handsome stranger had asked me to dance. I really didn't want to dance because it was country dancing and I didn't know how. But of course, since I was single and he was hot, all my "friends" shoved me out onto the dance floor with him. We single girls have all experienced this humiliation at least once. After embarrassing myself on the dance floor for a while for the entertainment of my friends, I realized that this handsome young stranger was actually a nice guy. Patient with my lack of dancing ability, anyway. We hung out for the rest of the evening in the bar, and exchanged numbers and made plans to try to see each other again before the weekend was over.

The next day we were texting back and forth all day and made plans to meet after our respective group activities were over for the evening. He was staying at the same hotel as some of the girls on our trip so I told him I'd meet him in that hotel's lobby bar. He wasn't there when I got there so I made two of my LTMFs sit with me until he got there, in case he *didn't* get there. They both confessed to me that they were so dang jealous that I was getting ready to potentially hook up with this young stud. They talked about how exciting it was and how adventurous. They told me how lucky I was. Lucky?! Are you completely cray? I agreed that it was fun and exciting, but told them that I would give all that up to have what they had – stable, long-term relationships. I was then pelted with a barrage of reasons from them on why being single is so much better than being in a relationship.

HERE I WAS SPENDING EVERY DAY AT THAT TIME IN MY LIFE BEING JEALOUS OF THE LTMFs, WHILE THEY WERE SPENDING THEIR TIME BEING JEALOUS OF ME!

What single women fail to realize is that being single is cool. It's damn cool! It's just as cool, if not cooler, than being in a committed relationship. See, your married friends know this. The reason they sometimes look down on your singleness is because they have jealousy of your situation, in the same way that you have jealousy of theirs. I'm reminded of the term "smug marrieds" from the Bridgette Jones's Diary books. And if you're not only single, but single and happy, single and livin' it up, single and free to do whatever (and whomever!) you want, then you're like the prom queen that every married loves to hate. Not only that, you've accomplished something that they haven't. You're getting through life on your own and you're doing it like a rock star. You're earning your own money, taking care of your own home, going on your own vacations, and doing it all just exactly the way YOU want to! Society wants you to feel that you're not allowed to be happy as a single person. Because if you are then you've done something that they either believed they couldn't do or simply wouldn't do. You're bucking the system. So, the next time you're sitting on the couch on Valentine's Day, eating chocolates from a mockingly heart-shaped box, and watching movies on the Hallmark channel, remember that nobody's life looks like those movies, not even the happiest of married people.

THE WORK

1. In what ways do you think of yourself as not belonging because you're single?

2. In what ways do you believe life is harder for you because you're single?

3. Are these facts or just things you've told yourself over and over? Rewrite each statement from the opposite viewpoint.

4. Write the following statement ten times: "I'm single and therefore I'm incredibly cool. I get to do what I want, when I want, and how I want, and people are jealous of that!"

CHAPTER 10

AWFUL, UNTRUE, LIMITING THOUGHT #9:
"LIFE BEGINS WHEN MY RELATIONSHIP BEGINS"

A lot of us put our lives on hold until Prince Charming comes galloping up on his mighty steed and gives us that kiss that changes everything for the better. I had a single friend who really wanted to buy a house, but she bought a townhome instead, saying that she'd buy a house when her husband came along because they would do that together. But you really want a house, right, not a townhome? Yes. And you're already annoyed at the neighbor noise you can hear coming though the walls? Yes. So, why don't you just buy a house already? Because it's something I want to do with my husband, not by myself. So, you don't want to be happy with your living situation until (if!) you have a husband? Uhhh...

Putting your happiness on hold until you have someone in your life is a dangerous proposition. First, you don't believe you can have ultimate happiness unless you have someone. Second, you're telling yourself that you're not worth ultimate happiness until someone comes along. And third, what if no one ever does? Now, it's unlikely that you'll never meet another potential suitor ever again, but what if the RIGHT one never comes along? Are you going to continue to live in that townhome with the base from your neighbor's stereo about to drum you into a murderous rage, or are you going to have the life you want to have right now, regardless of your relationship status on Facebook?

Being single doesn't make you less of a person and it doesn't doom you to a life of less than what you truly want.

ANYTHING YOU WANT YOU CAN HAVE AS A SINGLE PERSON AND YOU DO NOT NEED TO PUT ANYTHING ON HOLD.

You want a house? Buy a house! You don't want to do the yard work? Hire the kid down the street. You want a baby, have one. Or better yet, adopt one. There are so many lovable kids out there just waiting for a wonderful home like yours. Plus, then you don't have to be pregnant and turn your body inside out. Unless you want to. Not here to judge nature.

So often we have these images in our minds of how we want things to be. We want a house, but we want it with HIM. We want kids, but we want HIM in the family photos. We want to throw parties, but we want HIM to entertain the guests while we replenish the toast points. But these images are the same as the wealthy thirty-year old couple in the Christmas commercial with their matching watches and cars. They're ideal. But they're not necessarily real. And when we start to create new images in our heads of how life can be, based on our current reality, we can come up with some pretty satisfying stuff.

Before I embarked on my journey to Single Girl Bliss, I literally sat down and wrote out what my ideal life looked like. It went something like this. I start my own business with the help of my loving husband, who also pays the bills while I'm getting things off the ground. Once established, we buy our dream home together, where we live in wedded bliss. We furnish it with beautiful pieces that we both love and we entertain on a regular basis. We also travel several times a year and have the most wonderful time together. He makes sure there are always fresh flowers on the table for me. Not to mention the matching watches and cars in the perfectly landscaped driveway.

Then I rewrote the story, this time with me all on my own. I start my own business with the help of a friend and while I struggle to make ends meet at first, it makes the journey all the more rewarding. I buy my dream home, which is perfect just for me and the cats, and furnish it with beautiful pieces that have meaning for me. I start entertaining in my home, too. I start small, with just a few people, and eventually throw larger parties, enlisting the help of friends when necessary. I travel several times a year, either with friends or on my own, and my experiences have been some of the best of my life. I purchase fresh flowers for myself and enjoy picking out something new every week. I don't wear a watch and I only need one car!

AND JUST LIKE THAT I REALIZED THAT IT'S TOTALLY POSSIBLE TO HAVE THE LIFE OF MY DREAMS ALL ON MY OWN.

Being blissfully single doesn't have to be about giving up on the possibility of romantic love ever coming your way, but it does have to be about you living the life you want right now and not waiting for someone to bring your ideal life to you. I once met a lady who was down in the dumps because she just couldn't find a boyfriend. I decided I would do my best to help, so I asked her what she was looking for. She started rattling off her wish list and then she said, "I want someone who plays golf." Oh, so you're a golfer? No, but I want someone who plays golf. Well, do you have any interest in golf? Do you want to learn to play? I think so. After he comes along. Whaaat?! If you're interested in golf and you want to learn to play, why are you waiting for a golfer-Frog to come along before you do it? You can take lessons and join a ladies league all on your own. And when Golf Frog does come around, won't he be even more interested in someone who already plays and shares that interest with him?

Think of your single life like a vacation. Do you sit in the hotel room the whole time or do you get out there and do everything there is to do? While it may be scary to try new things on your own, especially if you've never done them before and have no idea if you'll be any good at them, it's also extremely liberating to know that you have the option. You don't have to wait for a Frog to come along and help you. Find a friend who's into what you're interested in doing and ask her to help you get started. Find a club that welcomes beginners and offers instruction and support. Put on your big girl panties, and get out of that hotel room and onto the zip-line. There are so many things to experience in life and the last thing you want to do is experience years of waiting for those experiences to happen.

THE WORK

1. In what ways have you put your happiness on hold until "someone comes along?" What things have you not done for yourself or by yourself because you're waiting for that someone?

2. Write out your ideal future story with having the man of your dreams come along tomorrow. The story where you get everything you want in life.

3. Now write out that same story where you get the same ideal life, but this time no one comes along and you get it all on your own. Do you now see how this is entirely possible?

4. What thoughts can you change to start seeing your life in terms of "I" and not "we?"

5. Write the following statement ten times: "I live a happy, amazing, enviable life regardless of my relationship status!"

CHAPTER 11

AWFUL, UNTRUE, LIMITING THOUGHT #10: "I DON'T WANT TO BE HAPPY SINGLE"

L et me tell you a little story about this particular limiting thought. Many years ago I broke up with Frog #27 not long before Christmas. I was devastated, as always, even though Frog #27 didn't even deserve to be on the same planet as me. I gathered up all of the stuff that he had left at my house, including every gift he had ever given me (the pile was small), stuffed it all into a bag, and unceremoniously dumped it on his doorstep one day. That year, I went to my parents' house for Christmas. My mom gave me the book, "Chicken Soup for the Single's Soul." Like the other Chicken Soup books, it's a compilation of short stories by various authors. I found this book to be quite comforting and have read it many times over the years.

But the very first chapter in the book is something I avoided like the plague, even the first time I read it. It's called "Single and Happy." What? Single and happy? I don't want to be single and happy, I want to be married and happy. When all I'm looking to do is get into another, better relationship, why in the world would I want to read about being single and happy? Besides, those two things are mutually exclusive. In other words, you can't have one AND have the other. Or so I thought. So, I skipped over that chapter entirely, not daring to read just one of the stories within or even ponder the title of the chapter for too long. I went on to the dating chapters, the single-again chapters, and the doing stuff for others chapters.

I'm not sure when I actually let myself delve into chapter one. It could've been after my breakup with Frog #38 when I pretty much decided I was NEVER going to find Prince Charming, even though that didn't call off The Endless Search entirely. What I found in that forbidden chapter was hope.

HERE WERE THE STORIES OF SEVERAL PEOPLE WHO TRULY WERE HAPPY BEING SINGLE.

Some of them chose to be single, while others were more or less thrust into it by playing relationship musical chairs over the years and coming up the last man/woman standing every time, like me. I still hadn't given myself over completely to being happy on my own, but it was comforting to know that there were others out there who had and they were doing just fine.

Several years later when I finally decided that being single and happy was the thing for me, I revisited chapter one. Now, not only did I find hope in those pages, I found kindred spirits, people who GOT IT, people who didn't believe that they would die if they didn't find someone or would at least end up a miserable, lonely old spinster. They had given up The Endless Search as I was doing and were reaping the liberation of letting it all go. I still read that book from time to time and chapter one is one of the only chapters I read. I'm still interested in doing stuff for others and I find the single-again chapter comforting, but I skip completely over the dating chapter. What? Dating? When I'm so happy on my own, why in the world would I want to read about dating?

The moral of this story is that if we're afraid to put out into the Universe our desire to be happy on our own because we believe that we'll then be committing to a life of abject alone-ness, all we're telling the Universe is that we don't want to be happy. If we're afraid to read chapter one because we don't even want to entertain thoughts of being happily single, then we're putting in an order for fried misery sandwiched between slices of relationships.

WOULDN'T IT BE BETTER TO TELL THE UNIVERSE THAT YOU WANT TO BE HAPPY NO MATTER WHAT?

That you want to find your Single Girl Bliss and that if someday that gets interrupted by Frog-turned-Prince-Charming, you want to be happy then, too? By telling the Universe that you want to be happy on your own you're not dooming your life to a series of RSVPs with no +1, the only thing you're ordering up is a great life right now. With a side of fries, please.

My suggestion is to make a life plan for yourself on your own. Make a Single Girl Bliss plan and be committed to fulfilling that plan for yourself so that you can have the things you want in life. I've said before that you need to order up what you want from the Universe and that you need to be very specific. Then you need to focus your thoughts on what you're ordering up and take action to make it so. So, if you order up a happy single life, does that mean you're telling the Universe that you're totally committed to being single? No, of course not. Being single is your circumstance. You're not focused on being single, you just are. What you're focused on is creating the thoughts and beliefs that will create the mindset of being happy. Then taking the actions to create your best life. You just happen to be single while doing this. It doesn't doom you to a life of singleness. In fact, it creates a life for you in which you're so happy that how could the Frogs not want to get with that? Then, if you decide one day that one of the Frogs is worthy of your magical kiss you'll be happily ready to receive your prince. And if not, then you'll be damn happy on your own and let me tell you, it's an awesome way to be!

Creating your Single Girl Bliss life and being happy on your own doesn't mean you can't *want* a relationship, it just means that you won't *need* it. And when you don't need it then you're free to enjoy your life as it is right now instead of focusing on some future relationship that doesn't yet exist. Even if what you truly want deep down in the depths of your soul is a mate for that soul, wouldn't it be better to be happy on your own right now? Because you can count on that. Remember, another person can't fill what's missing in your life and can't *make* you happy. Don't be afraid to tell the Universe that you want to be happy while single. The Universe has already decided that you're going to be single right now, right? Okay, Universe, then I'm ordering up the blue plate special of happiness to go with my singledom, and I expect nothing less, ya biatch. No, I don't recommend calling the Universe a biatch, even though she may seem so at times. Figure out exactly what it is that's going to make you happy, right here, right now, to-day. It's already on the menu, just waiting for you to put your glasses on and order it up.

THE WORK

1. Have you been afraid to accept being alone or start living your best life on your own because you're afraid that the Universe will think you're happy that you're single and never send you someone? What are your thoughts surrounding this?

2. Even if your ultimate goal is still to find a happy relationship someday, can you agree with the statement that it's better to be happy alone than be miserable with someone?

3. Write down all of the things you're going to ask the Universe to bring into your life that have nothing to do with a relationship.

4. Write the following statement ten times: "I deserve to be happy in a relationship. I also deserve to be happy on my own. I just deserve to be happy and live my best life always!"

CHAPTER 12

YOU HAVE EVERYTHING YOU NEED RIGHT NOW

Those ten limiting beliefs were pretty eye opening, weren't they? And I'm sure you've thought of others, as well. Good! Changing your thinking about being single is what's going to set you free. I know I've shown you how to do this, but I want to make sure you know that it isn't going to be easy. If you've carried around these beliefs for a long, long time, they're not just going to disappear because you're now aware of them. You're going to have to work to think in a new way and continue to do that work as you go through the next weeks, months, maybe even years. It's going to be hard, but it's going to be worth it. You will get there, I promise you that. You will start seeing your singleness in a whole new way.

We've all been exposed to the fairytales. The ones that were read to us as children by well-meaning parents as they tucked us into bed and off to dreamland. Girl is alone and lonely. Or worse yet, she's being held captive by an evil step-parent or forced into some kind of slave labor. Boy comes along and rescues her from her loneliness/captivity/days of scrubbing floors on her hands and knees. And they live happily ever after. But these books never actually went into what the "happily ever after" looked like, did they?

These fairytales seemed sweet and innocent enough. Wouldn't it be great if someone would come along and save us from all of our suffering? That just one kiss from his perfect, manly lips would rescue us from the captivity of our cubicles, melt away twenty pounds from our thighs, and transform our ill-fitting Kohl's outfits into something fresh from the Gucci showroom. Then we'd be carried off to his castle in the sky. Where we'd end up scrubbing floors on our hands and knees while he's off tipping a pint with the boys. Oops, that's never going to make the fairytales!

Expecting a relationship to come along and make you happy is no different than expecting anything else to come along and make you happy. Nothing outside of yourself can MAKE you happy.

IT'S UP TO YOU TO MAKE YOURSELF HAPPY, AND YOU AND ONLY YOU CAN DO THIS.

I spent years thinking that if the right guy would just come along then everything would be great. Somehow having this person in my life would make everything else that was "wrong" in my life suddenly better. I used to tearfully beg and plead with the Universe to please make whatever Frog I was currently with turn into my Prince so that The Endless Search could finally be over. Had that wish been granted, I could have ended up with any one of the Frogs I dated and life would've been okay, maybe even pretty good, but it wouldn't have been great. When you look back on your life, are "okay" and "pretty good" good enough, or do you want great? Now is not the time to put on hold any plans of making your life better on your own because you believe that when HE comes along all will be well.

Now, as I've said before, I'm not saying that being in a loving, committed, mutually respectful relationship can't enhance the life you're living. Of course it can. Very much so. IF it's a loving, committed, mutually respectful relationship. Even then it can't solve all of your problems. It can't make your boss stop being an idiot. It can't smooth your cellulite. And it can't make your mother mind her own damn business already! While a great relationship can do many things for you, it can't turn you into the person you want to be. No, I'm definitely not saying give up on love. I'm not saying give up on the idea of sharing your life with someone you feel like you've known your whole life and who you love so much sometimes it's overwhelming. I'm saying give up The Endless Search. The Search is torturous. The Search sucks the life right out of you. And the Search is pointless because if you're going to find someone then it'll happen regardless of The Search. How much longer are you going to go on living a life you're not happy with simply because you believe that it's not right without a man in it so you're loathe to give up The Search? Months? Years? The time to get the life you want is right now. So give up searching and start living!

ARE YOU A "DESPERATELY SEARCHING FOR LOVE" GIRL, OR ARE YOU A "LIVING A KICK-ASS LIFE" GIRL?

The point I was trying to drive home by exposing all of our awful, untrue, limiting thoughts is that those thoughts are what are keeping us bound in unhappiness, not our lack of Frog-turned-Prince. So, what sets us free, then? Changing those thoughts! Changing our beliefs around being single. Changing our mindset about who we are and what we want for our lives. And changing our actions so that we start living our happiest, best lives. You have everything you need to do this right here and right now. You know that the Universe exists and that you have a relationship with it, whether or not you've been tending to that relationship. You know that the Universe is waiting for you to order up the life you want. You know that in order to change your life, you only have to change your thinking. And you know that the actions that result from that change in thinking are what's going to create your best life. How amazing is it to now know this?

People think they're the best versions of themselves when they're in a relationship. "You complete me," and "You make me want to be a better person," are lines that have perpetuated this belief. Which is why it's so difficult for us to picture a happy life without a relationship. How can we possibly live our best lives on our own? But the opposite can actually be true. You can create your best life and live the best version of yourself while on your own. How's that, you ask? It's because instead of relying on someone else to provide you with the life you want, giving away all that power, and then being disappointed when they can't or won't do it, you have all the power to create exactly the life you want.

YOU ARE NOT NOBODY UNTIL SOMEBODY LOVES YOU.

YOU ARE SOMEBODY ALL ON YOUR OWN, YOU JUST HAVE TO FIGURE OUT WHO THAT PERSON IS.

It starts with shifting your thinking and focusing on yourself, then determining exactly who it is that you are. Not who you were in that relationship with Frog #7, but who you are on your own, as an individual. When you're in a relationship it's easy to lose sight of exactly who you are because you're someone else's someone. My brother and sister-in-law met in college, got married right after graduation, and have been together for nearly thirty years. They've dealt with some adversity in their family situation, but for all intents and purposes seem pretty happy. However, neither of them has any idea who they are separate from each other because they haven't been separate from each other since they were very young adults. There's nothing wrong with this, as they've created an identity as a couple and they're happy with it. It's not that they don't have their own individual interests or lead their own lives either, but I have a sneaking suspicion that neither of them is leading their most authentic life. They've never had a reason to even determine what that is, much less lead it. But you, my single friend, do!

This is the point where you wonder why you can't have your cake and eat it, too. Isn't it possible to be in a relationship and be living your authentic best life at the same time? Of course it is. But you have to be happy with yourself before you can be happy with someone else. Cliché, but true. So, what if God came down from the heavens and told you that you were definitely going to meet Mr. Right, but not for another ten years? Or twenty years? Would you wallow in self-pity that whole time? No, of course not. You'd get out there and live the best life you possibly could, and become the best person you possibly could so that when Mr. Right finally appeared you'd knock his socks off! I used to say to myself, "If I just knew when he was coming, I could relax and enjoy the time until he got here." So, what I was saying was that I couldn't enjoy life unless I knew for sure someone would come along one day? Gurl, please! Is that any way to live? Relax and enjoy the time NOW! If you need to tell yourself that he's coming next year or in five years or in ten in order to get yourself there, then do. Because one of two things is going to happen if you do things right. Either he actually will come along and you'll be all ready for him. Or he won't and you won't care. That's the beauty of living YOUR life for YOURself. The law of averages says that you're probably going to end up with someone. But it's your duty in the meantime to be as happy as you can be, which will in turn ensure that you end up with the right someone, should that mission arise and should you choose to accept it. Living best life = attracting best mate.

I had a friend once who had been married for thirty years and found herself divorced and alone one day. She wallowed in her aloneness for an entire year instead of taking charge of her life. One day a man asked her out and she accepted even though she knew he wasn't what she was looking for. They spent three years together before she inevitably dumped him because, you guessed it, he wasn't what she was looking for. When I asked her why she ever went out with him in the first place she told me it was because she wasn't in a position to turn down an invitation. What?!!! Don't be so grateful to be selected, ladies, be selective. This means spending some time on your own creating a happy life for yourself. And if you do, and if you get comfortable with who you are, and if you learn to enjoy your own company, and if you're truly happy, you'll be in a position to respect your own wishes for what you want in a mate.

How is it even possible to enjoy waiting for something to come along that makes your life better? How do you even know when or if this thing is going to come along? The waiting, the longing, the hoping, the doubt, none of this is fun. So stop waiting! You're not waiting for anything. You're living the best, happiest, most fulfilling life you can with the circumstances that you're in right now. Know that if something comes along one day to change those circumstances, at least you didn't waste your life waiting around for it. You don't want to ever say this to yourself, "While I was single I wish I would have..." Because once you're not single anymore, if that's what you choose, there's no going back. Hopefully. So live that best life NOW! What're you waiting for?

What I'm trying to get at here is that you have two choices: you can continue The Endless Search for Soulmate 1.0 or 2.0 or 9.0 or whatever version you happen to be on. You can spend all of your time and energy continuing that search. Or you can put that time and energy into living your best life. Now, what do I mean by best life when your best life up until now was defined by you having a man? What I mean by best life is the happiest life you can live within the circumstances that you currently have. So, for me, does living my best life mean becoming a super model? Let's see, I'm 47, I'm 5'9", I'm a size... well I'm far from a size 0, let's put it that way, and I wasn't blessed with the face of an angel, so you tell me. Is being a supermodel even possible in my current best life? Um, no. So, if you currently don't have a man in your life then living your best life right now doesn't include a man. So, what does living your best life right now look like?

SET AN INTENTION OF WHO YOU WANT TO BE AS A SINGLE PERSON.

It doesn't have to be the same, it shouldn't be the same, as who you are in a relationship. Relationships always mean compromising who we are to a certain extent. Always. Sometimes those compromises are worth it and sometimes they aren't. But you, lucky single girl, don't have to compromise at all. You can have whatever life you want. You're used to thinking in terms of "we" because we is what you've convinced yourself you want (need!) and we is what you had a month ago or a year ago or whatever. Let me clue you in on a little secret. The longer you spend alone the more you stop thinking in terms of the we that doesn't exist and start thinking in terms of the I that does.

When you're single, like no other time your life, you can be anything you want to be. I didn't think I could have my own interior design business until I found a man. I knew that starting a business would cost money and that there wouldn't likely be a lot of income at first. I needed someone else to pay the bills while I did this. And friends and family encouraged this belief. I know that they were just trying to look out for my best interests, but it certainly didn't help me have the confidence to do what I really wanted to do. So I kept working jobs I hated that paid the bills well and resigned myself to the fact that I wouldn't have a design business until I got married.

As time wore on and it looked like maybe I'd never get married, I decided it was now or never. I saved up some money, left my job, and started my business. And while I never achieved huge financial success as an interior designer, I did what I really wanted to do, helped a lot of people, and was able to stay afloat for more than four years until helping single women revealed itself as my true calling. Clearly, I didn't think I would be able to accomplish my goal, but I did, and the best part is I did it all on my own.

Several years ago I laid it all out on the table and created my own plan for living a Single Girl Bliss-ful life. In Part 2 of this book I'm going to show you how to create your own plan for living your happiest, best life right now. Are you ready to stop feeling alone and start feeling alive? Then turn the page, soon-to-be blissful single girl!

THE WORK

1. Write the following statement ten times: "I'm ready to live my happiest, best life ever!"

- Part 2 -

GETTING YOUR LIFE RIGHT

CHAPTER 13

WHO ARE YOU REALLY?

Now that we've talked about all of the limiting beliefs that are swirling around in our pretty little heads and we've learned how to combat these thoughts, we're going to get into the action-packed portion of achieving our Single Girl Bliss. In other words, I'm going to show you how to give up The Endless Search, define who you are, make a plan for your life and take action on that plan. With my help you're going to be able to create "Your Life 2.0." Woo-hoo! The biggest question you need to ask yourself is, "IF I were to spend the rest of my life alone, what does that look like?" Or maybe just the next five years or next ten years.

WHO ARE YOU, NOT AS SOMEONE WHO'S IN A RELATIONSHIP, NOT AS SOMEONE WHO'S EMBROILED IN THE ENDLESS SEARCH, BUT AS SOMEONE WITH THE ABILITY AND THE OPPORTUNITY TO CREATE AN AMAZING LIFE FOR YOURSELF?

Step one in figuring out who you are, what you want, and how to live happily ever after with yourself, is to give up The Endless Search. Yes, that's right, you gotta take down those online dating profiles and cancel your "It's Just Lunch" membership. Now, I know I'm going to get some resistance on this one because you're going to tell me that there's no harm in just seeing what's out there. But remember what I said about what you focus on and what you put out there into the Universe being what comes back to you? So, by continuing to cast your line into the pond just to see if something bites, are you focused on the party that's taking shape on shore? What you're saying to the Universe by continuing to be "out there" even if you're not actively pursuing anything is that you have a scarcity in your life that needs to be filled. And that scarcity mindset is only going to attract more scarcity instead of providing you with the fulfillment that you truly desire. Like attracts like, remember?

Some of you have been searching for someone for so long that you don't even know how not to. You don't even recognize not doing this as an option for you. It's a habit, something you just do. You've never even considered giving it up because it's just a part of who you are. You're going to have to change this habit. Are you even truly interested in finding someone anymore? Do you even know what that someone looks like? Or is it something that you just feel compelled to do on a daily basis without even thinking about it, like eating or brushing your teeth? Make a commitment to yourself to give up The Endless Search. You don't have to give it up forever. If at some point you decide that you want to get back into that game, you always can, it's always going to be there. I told myself I was going to give up The Endless Search for six months. I figured that's how long it would take me to take stock of my life, realize all of the great things about being single, and start treating myself well. That was really all I wanted at that point. I just wanted to be okay being single so that I would make much better relationship choices going forward. Then six months turned into a year and after that I was living such a wonderful, fulfilled life on my own that I never went back to The Endless Search.

Just in case some of you are getting really scared that you're going to have to give up on ever finding love in order to find happiness on your own, I want to reiterate that this is not the case. While I am now living my happiest, best life ever and have completely given up The Endless Search never to be seen or heard from again, I still haven't 100% closed the door on the possibility that one day a wonderful relationship could come along. Anything can happen, right? Is that scenario so far out of the realm of possibility? Well, if you took a look at my 21-year dating life you might think so, but no, of course it's not out of the realm of possibility. I just don't NEED it to happen anymore. I'm living my best life right now and not only am I "okay being single," I'm actually thriving as a single woman and the envy of many.

When you finally make the decision to give up The Endless Search there's a certain relief that flows over you. Of course there's fear, too, because any time we make a change in our lives, especially a big mental shift, there's going to be fear. Fear is our brain trying to save us from the imminent disaster that could come from making any sort of change in our lives. Remember, our brains don't like change. They want to keep us safe and alive, and how we're living right now is doing that, so why in the world would it want to change? Your brain wants you to continue The Endless Search because it's comfortable, it's what you've been doing for years and years, and it hasn't killed you yet. When you tell your brain to suck it and choose to give up The Endless Search or at least put it on hold, you will be amazed at the relief you feel once you get past the fear. And you will get past the fear. Your brain will adjust to this change just like it's adjusted to every other change you've ever made in your life.

The amazing relief comes when you realize that you no longer have to be bothered with any of the anxieties that come along with The Endless Search. No more wondering if your nose looks too big in your profile picture. No more spending your precious time checking in twenty times daily to see if anyone's swiped right. No more making escape plans in anticipation of an overly awkward first date. No more spending an hour on your hair with the hopes that just maybe you'll meet someone while out for happy hour with the girls. And no more holding uncomfortable poses that make your feet go numb so that your thigh fat won't goosh over the edges of your bar stool.

WHEN YOU GIVE UP THE ENDLESS SEARCH, YOU GET TO BE YOU.

JUST YOU.

You get to focus all the thoughts you previously focused on finding Mr. Right onto yourself instead and living your best life. Just think about the productivity you're going to create in your own life when you have all of this time and mental energy to devote to it. You go, single girl!

So, are you ready to give up The Endless Search? At least for a little while? If the answer is no, I gotta keep searching, gotta keep at it, can't let go of finding someone, let me ask you this: Are you willing to keep searching and searching and making yourself and your life miserable, when you could be doing something to make yourself happy? If not, here's what you have to do. Take down your online dating profiles and/or cancel your memberships. Stop attending singles functions, unless you're truly there to make friends or participate in an activity. Stop asking people to set you up with someone. And stop agreeing to be set up when someone suggests it. Unless the person sounds completely and totally amazing and perfect and looks like George Clooney, but what are the odds of that? Stop attending every function looking like a glamour shot. If you truly want to get all dolled up for wine with the girls because that's just who you are, then by all means continue, but if you're doing it because you're thinking you might attract someone, just stop. Stop your thoughts on meeting someone, finding someone, being with someone. You're done with all of that for a while. Start letting people know that you're off the market for a bit. Start looking at every event you attend as an opportunity to spend time with friends or make new ones and experience whatever activity that event is about, instead of constantly scanning the room for Brad Pitt look-alikes.

The Endless Search is like a dating hamster wheel. You're going and going and going and putting all of your heart and soul and energy into this endeavor, but never reaching your destination. At some point you've got to wake up and say what the hell am I doing? This isn't serving me! When you do this, when you truly commit yourself to giving up The Endless Search, at least for a while, you will free yourself up to start searching for yourself instead. Who are you? What do you want? How do you want your life to be? And how are you going to get this for yourself? It's not the old cliché of "finding yourself."

LIFE IS NOT ABOUT FINDING YOURSELF, IT'S ABOUT CREATING YOURSELF, AND IT REALLY IS WHAT YOU NEED TO DO.

We spend so much time defining ourselves as who we are in a relationship, even if that relationship exists only in our heads. It's time for you to own your alone and live your best life. Right now. As a single woman. So, what does that look like?

The second step in figuring out how to live happily ever after with yourself, is to figure out exactly who "yourself" is. The most important thing you need to do in defining yourself is to accept yourself as you are right now, which includes accepting that you're single. This is how you are right now. There's nothing wrong with it. You're perfectly okay. Now, this doesn't mean that you won't have things about yourself that you want to change, but it means that by accepting yourself you also accept that you alone have the power to change yourself and your life for the better. You've heard it said that the happiest people on Earth are the ones who want what they already have. Try wanting to be single. How can I possibly do that, you ask? Just try. That's what I did. I decided I was going to take a break from wanting to meet someone and thereby gave up The Endless Search. I made the choice to be completely single for a while. Then I changed my thoughts and figured out how to think as a single person who's happy with her life the way it is. You need to define what your life looks like without a man in it. But isn't that the life you're living right now? Yes, but it's not defined and it's not happy. Shifting your focus to being happy on your own and figuring out what that looks like is key.

Once you change your thoughts about being single you'll start to think about life differently. You'll start to view things in a different way and you'll do different things that will change your life for the better. You'll then be able to craft the life you want, with the career, home, people and activities you want in it. If all of this sounds about as easy as scaling Mount Everest, never fear. I'm going to show you how to do all of this in the following chapters.

THE IMPORTANT PART IS THAT YOU ACCEPT YOURSELF FOR THE KICK-ASS WOMAN THAT YOU ARE, AND YOU ACCEPT YOUR SINGLENESS FOR THE AMAZING OPPORTUNITY THAT IT IS!

So, why is it so important that you accept yourself as you are right now? It's because as you begin your journey to Single Girl Bliss you're going to need a friend to help you, and that friend is you. You must find true friendship within yourself and you do this by accepting yourself completely. The people that we're closest to, who we enjoy spending time with the most and who are there for us to lean on, are the people whom we've accepted completely the way they are. Sure, you may wish that your BFF was capable of meeting you someplace on time. Ever. Just once, even. You may wish that your sister would respond to your texts in less than 24 hours instead of leaving you wondering whether or not she's still alive. There may in fact be many things about the people who are important to you that bug you and that you wish would change, but you've accepted that they probably won't and you love them anyway. You need to make friends with yourself, and eventually have the same unconditional love for yourself as you do for your loved ones.

This doesn't sound super difficult, right? Okay, I just accept myself the way I am and know that I have the power to change anything I want when I get to that point. But it's not really that easy. The reason it's not that easy is that we all have stories that we've written for ourselves. We have stories about our childhoods, how our parents and siblings treated us, how our teachers reacted to us, what our friends said about us, who wanted to date us and who didn't, how our romantic relationships worked out, etc. What you make your story mean about you determines who you think you are, your story alone does not. Huh? Okay, let me give you a little example of what I mean.

My own personal romantic story was one filled with lots of rejection. I can remember as far back as middle school having crushes on boys who most certainly did not return the affection. High school wasn't much better. When I met my ex-husband during the summer after high school and he actually seemed to be into me, I glommed onto him like a bear on a trash can. We were married a year later, which of course was a colossal mistake, and ultimately ended in even more and worse rejection. I actually left him, but it was because he was doing nothing to help make our relationship work. Read: rejection. Then came the 21 years of dating, relationships, and you guessed it – assloads of rejection! So, if I were going to take my romantic story at face value, what might I believe about myself? Well, probably that I wasn't worthy of a relationship. That there was something grossly wrong with me or many things, actually, and that I just wasn't lovable. That I was doomed to live a life of loveless spinsterhood. Is that what I want to believe about myself? Does that serve me? Does it make my life better in any way? No! As a matter of fact, it does the exact opposite. So, how can I take that same story and make it mean something different about me?

I can start by accepting that everything that has happened in my life up until now has happened the way it was supposed to and has made me the person that I am today. I am a strong person because I handled all of that rejection and came out swinging. I wouldn't be writing this book right now if any of those relationships had worked out. I wouldn't have the viewpoint that I have and wouldn't be able to share personal examples with you if I hadn't experienced what I've experienced. I wouldn't be a life coach who's helping single women every day if I hadn't been on the personal journey that I was on. In other words, I wouldn't be me! And I love me, so it's much better for me to make my story mean about me what I need it to mean in order to serve me well. You need to make your story mean about you something that serves you well, too. If you've had lots of heartache and rejection in your life, tell yourself that it's made you a stronger person. Because it has. Tell yourself that the time Frog #13 dumped you and you were devastated, and you're still devastated to this day, was because you're destined for something better than Frog #13. Tell yourself that all the time you've spent alone crying because you were just sure that you were never going to find anyone, has made you capable of actually spending time alone. Your story itself doesn't make you who you are.

ALL OF THE AMAZING THINGS THAT YOU MAKE YOUR STORY MEAN ABOUT YOU MAKE YOU WHO YOU ARE AND DETERMINE HOW YOU FEEL ABOUT YOURSELF.

Once you've accepted yourself for who you are right here and now, accepted your singleness, and accepted that your story can mean anything you want it to mean, you'll then be able to define who you are and where you want to be. Defining who you are as an individual outside of a relationship can be difficult. It means focusing entirely on yourself and not on who you are in relation to someone else. That's scary for a lot of people. At the same time, it's also completely liberating and empowering. Because not only do you get to define who you are right now, you also get to plot a course for who you want to be going forward. You get to become the person you want to be for YOU, not for someone else. You get to create "Your Life 2.0," with no waiting for someone else to come along. This should excite you at least as much as finding out your high school nemesis has gotten really, really fat. We all know that being in a relationship can be great, but it can also be not great. And we know that being alone can be not great, but it can also be really, really great. When you're on your own you're 100% in control of that greatness. When you're in a relationship you're at least 50% at the whim of the other person.

It's easy to feel a little lost at first when beginning this journey.

You've been biding your time, possibly for years, going through the motions until Perfect Man 38.0 came along to save you from your pathetic existence. What now? What now is exactly what we're going to talk about next. What you focus on you create more of. This sentiment is in all of the best self-development books, so I had to put it in my book, as well. But the reason it's in all of the books is that it's true, and I discussed it in more detail in the first part of this book. So, now that you've accepted yourself for who you are right now as a single woman, we're going to talk about what "who you are" really means and define what you want your life to be. You're going to focus 100% on yourself and create your best life, the life YOU truly want.

Figuring out where you want to be is much easier when you know where you are right now. This means looking at all of the different aspects of your life, not including romantic relationship, of course. You want to take a look at the following:

CAREER: Are you happy in your current job? Do you make the money you'd like to be making? Are you on a path for professional growth and development?

HOME: Do you like where you live? Is your home comfortable and reflective of who you are? Do you like your car, clothes, and other material possessions you have?

HEALTH & FITNESS: Do you have any health problems that need to be addressed? Are you happy with your weight? What about your current level of fitness? Are you happy with the way you eat and exercise on a daily basis?

FRIENDS & FAMILY: How are your relationships with your parents, children, siblings, extended family? What about your friendships? Are they loving and supportive? Do you feel that you have enough friendships?

PERSONAL DEVELOPMENT: Do you take steps to do the things in life that you want to do? Are you learning that new language, taking that photography class or finishing that degree? Are you getting to those books on your reading list?

RECREATION: Do you make time to do the things you enjoy doing? Have you signed up for that kayaking class? Are you planning that girls' weekend? Did you finish crocheting that afghan?

COMMUNITY: Do you support the causes that have meaning for you? Do you volunteer? Are you active in your neighborhood or church activities?

When you answer all of these questions and probably come up with even more on your own, that's when you start to define who you are. How you show up in life is who you are. So, if you have a great job that you love and pays you well, you live in a lovely home surrounded by lovely things, you work out and eat right every day, you have a loving, supportive family and slew of friends, you're constantly looking for ways to enrich yourself, you take part in recreation and hobbies whenever you can, and you give back to your community as much as possible, then chances are you're living your best life already. How many of us can say that we're doing all of these things? For a lot of us, some of these things have taken a backseat to make time for The Endless Search, or we just had the notion that they would get addressed once we were in a relationship. It's time to stop thinking that way and get your life on track, on your own, for you. You're in the unique position of being able to make your life 100% about you, cuz there ain't no one else! Now, of course, if you have young kids or you're taking care of an ailing parent or something, you obviously have to put certain needs of theirs above your own. In these cases your life simply can't be 100% about you and that's okay. These are your current circumstances and you can still create your best life within the parameters of these circumstances. Sometimes even taking a look at them will cause you to see that you can delegate some of that responsibility elsewhere or enlist some help so that you can get to the business of focusing on your own life.

Since you've now defined where you are, it should be fairly easy to see where you'd like to be. If you've realized that you hate your job and you make crap money, I'm sure that's not something you want for your life in the future. If your idea of working out is walking from the car into the donut shop, then I'm sure the health and fitness area of your life is less than working for you. No matter where your life is right now, it absolutely can get better starting right now, no romantic relationship required.

WHEN YOU'RE SINGLE YOU CAN CRAFT YOUR LIFE HOWEVER YOU WANT IT. YOU CAN CREATE THE EXACT LIFE YOU WANT BECAUSE NO ONE'S STANDING IN YOUR WAY. HOW POWERFUL IS THAT?

It's not just about creating a new life for yourself or creating a life, period, if you've never really had one before, it's about creating a lifeSTYLE! I remember once in my early 20's I went to a shi-shi hair salon with a friend of mine. Prior to that my idea of an expensive haircut was going to Supercuts instead of Great Clips. You didn't grow up in my household paying any more than $8 for a haircut. I have the pictures to prove it. So, here I was at this shi-shi salon getting my hair cut by a very hip, very gay stylist. My hair had been long and straight for years and since I have pretty thin hair, it was always kinda flat and scraggly, and I was sick of it. I told the stylist to just do something with it and what I got was the "Rachel." Remember the Rachel from the 90's? The style made famous by Jennifer Aniston of Friends? It was all layers and curves and volume and it looked amazing! My friend exclaimed, "Oh my God, she has HAIR!" And the stylist said with a flourish, in his perfectly rehearsed lisp, "No, she has a hairSTYLE!" What your road map to Single Girl Bliss will entail is you styling your life exactly the way you want it and making it better than anything you've ever had before. You're done with thin and scraggly, and you're ready for the Rachel!

So, how does one do this? It's too bad there aren't salons for your life. You walk in and tell them you're sick of your life and ask them to just do something with it, and you walk out with a brand new fabulous lifeSTYLE. Unfortunately it doesn't work that way and it's up to you instead. First of all, you gotta get rid of everything in your life that's not working – commitments, friends, whatever. You've identified how things are right now, so what out of all that isn't working? Your job? Your relationship with your mother? Your lack of any hobbies whatsoever? When you start living authentically (who you want to be) you not only create your best life, but you also boost your self-esteem and who couldn't use that? I know my fabulous new hairSTYLE certainly boosted mine and it was just hair. Imagine what a whole new life plan is going to do for you? Now, this doesn't mean that you have to change absolutely everything. If there are certain things that are working for you, great! Keep those things the same and work on the rest.

Aside from your new life plan, there's one other thing that you're going to have to start doing for yourself and that's treating yourself well. Maybe you already do this and if you do, kudos to you, but one of the biggest things I identified for myself after making the decision to give up The Endless Search and focus on myself was that I hadn't been treating myself very well. I was expecting the Frogs to come along and treat me well when I wasn't even capable of doing that for myself, nor did I really even know what that was. Treat yourself like a lady. Take yourself out on a date. Have your own dreams, goals and ambitions. Challenge yourself and reach for something greater than you've ever had. Buy yourself little gifts just because. Buy yourself flowers. These are not things you have to give up ever having again unless you're in a relationship. These are things that we should all be doing for ourselves on a regular basis. If it's hard for you to envision this, do a little exercise. Write down what you would do for a mate or a BFF to show them that they're loved and appreciated. On holidays? Anniversaries? Birthdays? When they've accomplished something special? Just because? Now, write down what you want done for you on those same occasions. Okay, now go do those things for yourself!

Obviously, you're not going to be buying yourself flowers every day. Nor will you have the time or money to plan elaborate celebrations for yourself very often. So, what about the day to day?

How do you treat yourself well on a daily basis? When you're in a relationship, just having someone to come home to for a hug or someone to share dinner with can make you feel treated well, but it's more difficult when you're on your own. The best way to treat yourself well on the daily is to get excited about your day, even if the only things to get excited about are the cold pizza you're going to have for breakfast, the leftover Chinese takeout you're going to have for dinner, and the fact that the final season of Girlfriends Guide to Divorce has finally dropped on Netflix. We take these things for granted, but imagine if you didn't have food or a TV. These trivial things would be pretty special, right?

REALIZE ALL OF THE GOOD THINGS AROUND YOU ON A DAILY BASIS AND APPRECIATE THEM.

A little gratitude goes a long way to feeling like you're treating yourself well.

Now, you're likely to come across some things that you realize someone else used to do for you and now you have to do for yourself. You're also likely to look at a particular aspect of your life and realize that you never had to worry about that before because it was taken care of by someone else. These thoughts could make you a little bit sad. It felt good to have someone else do things for you, didn't it? It felt good to not have to worry about every little aspect of your life because someone else was responsible for some of it, right? It felt good to have someone care about you and therefore do things for you. But it's not about how you think someone else feels about you, it's about how that thought makes you feel about yourself. If someone gives you a dozen roses, the roses themselves or even the gesture doesn't make you happy, it's how the gesture makes you feel about yourself – I'm loved, I'm special, I'm worthy. So it stands to reason, then, that doing things for yourself will also make you feel good about yourself. In fact, they may make you feel even better. Those dozen roses given to you by a Frog may have been a feeble attempt to make up for being a complete asshat during an argument the day before. When you give them to yourself, there's been no asshattery, you're just loved, special and worthy.

One thing that's very important to remember as you're getting this all together is that you're not alone here. Just because you don't have a romantic relationship does not mean that you're alone. You have your family, you have your friends, you have your coworkers, and these people are there for you and want you to be happy. If they're not, then you've identified that in your take-stock and maybe it's time to clean house.

SURROUND YOURSELF WITH POSITIVE, SUPPORTIVE PEOPLE AND YOU CAN'T GO WRONG.

And by all means, enlist the help of these people. I'm not one to ask for help. It has always made me feel weak and indebted.

But you'll find that when you ask a positive, supportive person for help, and that person wants to help you, your bond will grow even stronger. You're not weak because you need help and you're not indebted, either. We all need help at some point or another and we need to be able to ask our fellow humans for that help. You enjoy helping others, right? They'll enjoy helping you, too.

You're also not the only one in the single girl boat. You always think that everyone else is in a relationship and you're the only one who's not. There are over 58 million single women just in the United States right now. So, obviously, you ain't the only one. And if you feel like you're the only one in your immediate circle, you may very well be. Own it! When all the LTMFs start whining about the fights they had with their husbands last night, say, "You know who I fought with last night? No one!" And then toss your hair back and laugh hysterically for effect.

As you embark on your journey to Single Girl Bliss, you're also likely to come across some thoughts and emotions that will try to derail you. The one that continually came up for me was, "There's no reason in the world that I should be single. There's no reason that I should have to create this life for myself all on my own. This wasn't part of the plan and I don't wanna!" How I got past this was by not thinking of it as a burden, but instead thinking of it as a gift. You GET to have the exact life that you want even if that life doesn't look like the one you originally imagined. How many people's lives do? How many people are living that fairytale dream they imagined as a kid? You're really in the same boat as everyone else. And you, single girl, have the unique advantage of being able to decide exactly what your best single life looks like and do what it takes to get it.

You're going to need to arm yourself with an action plan. You've determined where you are right now. You've determined where you want to be. You've decided you're going to start treating yourself well and stop thinking of your singleness as a burden. And you've recognized that you're not alone and you have people you can turn to for help. Now you need to figure out how to get from point A to point B. In the following chapters I break down each aspect of your life that I identified for you in your take-stock exercise and I go into more detail on how you can get those aspects in order. Remember, the first thing you have to do is change your thinking, that will then change your emotions, and your new positive emotions will cause you to take action toward your goal of creating your best life.

Before you start laying out your plan for your amazing new life, I want to address one aspect of life that may or may not affect you and that's children. I've touched on the topic a few times so far in this book, but part of the whole premise of this book is that you're focusing entirely on yourself and you're not going to be able to do that if you have young children. I recognize this fact. I'm not going to go into a lot of detail about things pertaining to kids or single parenting. There are many, many other resources out there for single moms that will do a much better job of this than I can. This book is primarily written for single girls with no kids or kids who are grown at least to the point of doing their own thing and not needing you for every little thing. I know your life plan is going to look different for you if you have kids, at least until they reach a certain age, and it's not going to be able to be 100% about you. That's okay, you can still change your thinking about being single and you can still change your life as a single woman. You're just going to have to take into consideration your children while you're doing so and make sure your plans take care of them, as well.

YOU'RE ABOUT TO CREATE YOUR PLAN FOR EMBARKING ON YOUR JOURNEY TO SINGLE GIRL BLISS AND I COULDN'T BE MORE EXCITED FOR YOU!

THE WORK

1. What fears do you have about giving up The Endless Search? Since fears are just thoughts, what counter-thoughts can you think in order to battle those fears?

2. What good things will come for you when you give up The Endless Search? More time for yourself? More money (no dating site fees)? Less angst?

3. What have you been making your story mean about you? In other words, what have the events of your past made you negatively believe about yourself?

4. Answer all of the following questions, if you haven't already:

   CAREER: Are you happy in your current job? Do you make the money you'd like to be making? Are you on a path for professional growth and development?

   HOME: Do you like where you live? Is your home comfortable and reflective of who you are? Do you like your car, clothes, and other material possessions you have?

   HEALTH & FITNESS: Do you have any health problems that need to be addressed? Are you happy with your weight? What about your current level of fitness? Are you happy with the way you eat and exercise on a daily basis?

FRIENDS & FAMILY: How are your relationships with your parents, children, siblings, extended family? What about your friendships? Are they loving and supportive? Do you feel that you have enough friendships?

PERSONAL DEVELOPMENT: Do you take steps to do the things in life that you want to do? Are you learning that new language, taking that photography class or finishing that degree? Are you getting to those books on your reading list?

RECREATION: Do you make time to do the things you enjoy doing? Have you signed up for that kayaking class? Are you planning that girls' weekend? Did you finish crocheting that afghan?

COMMUNITY: Do you support the causes that have meaning for you? Do you volunteer? Are you active in your neighborhood or church activities?

5. How can you start treating yourself well on a daily/weekly/monthly basis? This doesn't have to be anything major, it can be as simple as making sure your house is stocked with your favorite foods.

6. Write the following statement ten times: "I know who I am and I'm about to create a plan for who I want to be, which includes treating myself like the kick-ass person that I am!"

CHAPTER 14

CAREER

Now we're really going to get into the nitty-gritty of your life so that you can start to develop your plan for getting your life to where you want it to be. In the last chapter I had you think about all the different aspects of your life, where you are now and where you want to be. The first aspect is Career. Unless you were fortunate enough to be born into wealth or you've won the lottery or something, chances are you have a job of some kind. Even if you don't expressly need the money, you may have a job anyway, and since our jobs take up about a third of our working-age lives, they're worth focusing on.

As a single woman, your job can take on a different meaning than it maybe has for your married counterparts. For one thing, you're supporting yourself, with no second income to help out. That's not to say there aren't married women out there who are the sole income earner in their households and who are supporting a husband/boyfriend to boot, but usually a two-person household means a double income. Secondly, because you don't have a relationship to focus on, your job holds greater weight in your life. It's not only where you go for an income, it's where you go for friendship and comradery and achievement and validation. Sometimes your whole social life is anchored to your job. After I got divorced I moved to a new city where I knew no one. My first friends were coworkers and it was several years before I made any friends that I didn't work with. Not that married women can't be very connected to their jobs, but the single woman will place different meaning on her job than someone who has a relationship to focus on, as well.

I often say that there are three things in life that are the biggies, the most important things in anyone's life, and those three things are: 1. Your romantic relationship, 2. Your children, 3. Your job. Of course there are other important things, such as friends, other family, home, interests, etc, but these three things are the main things on which people focus the majority of their time. So, if you're single and you have no children, that leaves your job as the one big thing on which you focus.

WOW, THAT PUTS A LOT OF PRESSURE ON YOUR JOB TO BE SOMETHING THAT'S BOTH FULFILLING AND BRINGS IN A GOOD AMOUNT OF MONEY FOR YOU.

This doesn't mean that you have to LOVE your job, but you should at least like it, and loving it is so much better. Once I started my own business that I loved, it was much easier to be single because I was no longer looking for a man to "save me" from the jobs I hated and give me something else on which to focus. One of the three biggies was fulfilled instead of zero of three.

What if you're one of those women who likes/loves her job and makes plenty of money (your friends likely hate you), but your job so dominates your life that there's no way you can conceive of creating your best life as you defined it in the last chapter? Or maybe you're even using your job as a distraction so that you don't have to take a good look at who you truly are and what you truly want, or go to the trouble of creating your best life? This is a philosophical work-life balance question. If you want to create your best life and your best life doesn't consist of only working and never having time for anything else, then something's gotta give. You're going to need to find time for the other things in your life that are important to you and this may mean cutting back on your work time. If your job simply won't allow that then maybe finding a new job is in order. If you love this job then there will be another one out there that you'll love just as well and won't keep you from having the life that you want.

My mom used to love to come to my house and point out all of things that didn't measure up to her cleanliness standards. My ceiling fan blades had dust on them, my microwave had a few food splatters, and it looked like no one had washed the windows in years (cuz no one had!). This condescension came from a woman who had been a stay-at-home wife and mother, was now "retired," and could've spent every day of her life cleaning something if she wanted to. Meanwhile, I was working full time to support myself, in school at night to make a happier life for myself, and spent my weekends working on homework and catching up on sleep. After yet another comment on the cleanliness of my microwave, I said, "Mom, when I'm on my deathbed and I'm looking back at my life, am I going to wish I had had more fun or am I going to wish that I had cleaned more?!" No one ever wishes she had cleaned more. No one ever wishes she had worked more, either. Find a way to create work-life balance.

So, what do you do if you like/love your job and it doesn't dominate your entire existence, but the money just isn't there to get you to the life you truly want? The best thing you can do is ask for a raise. Women are usually grossly underpaid, and not just in comparison to our male counterparts, but in general. We don't ask for what we're worth when we accept a job in the first place and then we spend the rest of our time there trying to catch up, which we never really do. No one is going to hand you the money you deserve. You're going to have to research what others outside your company in similar positions are making. You're also going to have to identify how valuable you are to your organization. If you can't come up with your value then add some. Take some initiative and go above and beyond. When you're armed with the facts then you can ask for that raise with confidence. And you're likely going to get it. Companies don't like to lose valuable employees; it's expensive for them, and paying you a few extra thousand a year is not going to put them out of business. If you still can't score that raise then it may be time to weigh your happiness with your job against your happiness with life if you made more money. You might have to find someplace else to be happy – it's out there.

What do you do if you're single and your job is sucking your will to live? Even if the money's good. Trust me, I've been there. I've had jobs that were so stressful or so defeatist or so mind-numbingly boring that the negativity of them consumed my life and made me miserable. Now, of course, I also allowed these jobs to do this to me. Because remember that our thoughts are choices and I chose to think that my job was turning my life into an insidious sinkhole of despair. That said, you basically have two choices. You can change your thinking about your job or you can find a new one. The former seems like the easier thing to do, but not always.

IF THERE'S A TUGGING AT YOUR HEARTSTRINGS TO DO SOMETHING ELSE, THEN PURSUING THAT MAY BE THE EASIER CHOICE.

I spent a number of years in the corporate world as a buyer for several contract engineering and manufacturing firms. For the most part I was paid decently for what I did, I got benefits, and I was able to work in professional offices. But every time I would get a job with a new company in the field, the honeymoon phase would inevitably wear off after about 6 months and I'd be back to hating life. It's because I had virtually no interest in the projects the company was doing and only a marginal interest in my job, period. I wanted to do something else, but what was it?

After the honeymoon phase had worn off from job number four, I sat myself down and made myself really think about what I wanted to do with my life. Even though the money was pretty good, I knew I couldn't do what I was doing for the rest of my career, so I had to figure out something else. My brother once said to me when I was in my 20's and struggling to find my career "self," that you have to figure out what you love to do and then find a way to make money doing it. Such a simple yet profound statement that has stuck with me since he first said it. Keeping this statement in mind, I took a look at all the things I love to do and then decided which one of them I could see making a career out of. And that's how I became an interior designer.

Of course there was much more to it than that. I was single so I couldn't just quit my job and go back to school while my husband covered the bills for a while. I spent six years in design school working on a degree, attending classes part time in the evening while I continued to work full time during the day. And the whole time I was thinking, "How in the world am I going to start my own business? I won't be able to, I'm going to have to get married first." Because, as I'm sure you know, brand new businesses don't usually start raking in the dough right away and I had a mortgage to pay. Once I graduated and was still single I knew I couldn't start my own business, nor could I go to work for a firm making the kind of money that entry level interior designers are paid. So, I made a plan. I started by paying off my debt, which at the time was only a car note. I also reduced my expenses as much as possible. Once the car was paid off, I took that money and started saving it toward a slush fund to be used to help finance me once I started my interior design business. I created a "second income," if you will. Three years later I was able to leave my buying job and start my own business. I'm still reeling from the transition I made in my mind from can't-be-done to absolutely-can-be-done-with-a-little-planning. While I have now moved onto other things, such as this book, that experience showed me that where there's a will there's a way, regardless of your marital status.

For you, finding happiness in your career may not mean going out on a limb and starting your own business, it may just mean making a career change or even just a job change. Or it may mean changing your thinking about your job and making peace with it, especially if you like the company, your coworkers, and you get paid well. Either way, if you're not happy in your current job or career path for whatever reason, you need to do something about it. Creating your best life includes creating your best career since our jobs are so important to us as single women. There are so many options out there for you even if you don't believe there are. Remember, I thought starting my business as a single woman was out of the question, but it wasn't, I just had to change my thinking about it. Are we sensing a pattern here?

THE WORK

1. If you like/love your job and make enough money, but your job consumes your life leaving you with little time for anything else, what can you do to change this? Can you spend less time at work, hire someone to help, or is it time to bite the bullet and find a new job?

2. If you like/love your job, but you're not making enough money, what can you do to change this? Can you ask for a raise and/or add value to your company, or is it time to search for a new job-love?

3. If you hate your job and you're not making the kind of money you need, or even if the money's okay, then it's kind of a no-brainer that you need to find a new job. Make a list of the companies/jobs you'd like to target.

4. Write out the steps you need to take to get from point A (where you are now) to point B (where you want to be). This is your plan for getting your career in order.

CHAPTER 15

HOME

Before we get into the next aspect of your life – your home – that you need to take a look at and decide whether or not it's working for you, let's spend a little time talking about living alone. Living alone is difficult for a lot of people. It was difficult for me when I first started doing it. As I mentioned earlier in the book, while I was going through my divorce I moved to a new city where I knew no one. I rented an apartment and found myself living alone for the first time ever. I absolutely hated it! Not only was I scared half the time, but since I knew no one I didn't even have people to invite over or anyone inviting me to leave the house. It was just me and my cat sitting there staring at each other in a one-bedroom apartment. I was so lonely that every other weekend I would drive to my parents' house seventy-five miles away and spend the weekend with them. Soon I got used to living alone and it became okay, especially when I started to make friends and I wasn't just sitting at home alone all the time. Netflix didn't exist back then so you can imagine the horror! But not long after that I actually started to like living alone and now I completely love it! There are so many wonderful things about living alone just like there are so many wonderful things about being single. You just have to open your mind to those things and they will present themselves.

WONDERFUL THINGS ABOUT LIVING ALONE AS A WOMAN:

- You get to have a cat if you want
- The seat is always down
- You can fart whenever you want
- No playing couch commando with the remote
- No one eats your potato chips
- The closet is yours all yours
- There are no posters of sports figures or motorcycles gracing your walls
- The dishwasher gets loaded correctly every time (divorced ladies, you know what I mean)
- Your garage contains your car, not dirt bikes and ATVs
- You get the whooooole bed to yourself! (well, you still have to share it with the pets)

The list goes on and on, of course, but these are some of the highlights. Now, if you're one of those women who's afraid to live alone, I feel you. There are many precautions you can take, however, and I invite you to look at them all. Installing a security system should give you the peace of mind that you need. And since they all integrate to your smart-phone these days, you can also use it to watch the cats walk around on your kitchen counters while you're at work, which you've sworn to everyone you know that your little angels don't do. The fear will subside in time. Living alone may be new for you and like all changes there's a certain amount of fear that goes with it. Have a trusted friend, family member or neighbor that you can call if you're feeling especially afraid.

AS WITH THE BEAUTY OF BEING SINGLE, THE BEAUTY OF LIVING ALONE WILL LIKELY TAKE SOME TIME TO PRESENT ITSELF TO YOU. BE PATIENT AND BE ON THE LOOKOUT FOR ALL OF THE JOYS THAT LIVING ALONE BRINGS TO YOU.

Your home is another key part of your life that takes on a different meaning than it has for the married and cohabitating. For one thing, you have no need for a she-shed, your entire home is your she-shed and you get to do with it whatever you want. Secondly, you don't have to share. Now, if you have kids then obviously you're sharing your home with them, but they have their own rooms so you should be able to claim the rest of the house for your gloriously single self within a few kid-friendly parameters. When you're single and live alone your entire house becomes your "room." It has meaning for you and only you, and should reflect who you are as an individual. Think of it this way: no dead animal's head will ever grace your walls, unless you're into that sort of thing. You are the queen of your castle and the queen gets to set things up any way she wants.

Your home also provides comfort for you in a way that's different from your married counterparts. Not to say that married people can't derive comfort from their homes, but for the single person coming home after a long day in the office, there's not another person to provide comfort so the home has to do double duty. When you're enveloped by your four walls, those walls say "me," not "we," so they need to provide the specific comforts that you need.

YOU ARE IN THE UNIQUE POSITION TO BE ABLE TO DO WITH YOUR HOME WHATEVER YOU WANT.

When I was back in my Endless Search days I wanted nothing more than to decorate a home for "us." I would shop the home goods stores and imagine how "our" tastes would be perfectly aligned and picture the things "we" would select for "our" home. At the same time I had a friend who had divorced after 30 years of marriage. She wanted nothing more than to create a home of her own, surrounded only by things that she truly loved and wanted for herself. I got where she was coming from, but never truly understood it until I became an interior designer.

My vision of what it would be like to work with clients who were couples went something like this: Husband would pretend to be interested in the design process, but really wouldn't be, and/or would have no clue, so would just say that whatever Wife wanted was fine with him. Or maybe he'd be really honest and say that while he had an opinion he knew it didn't matter anyway and whatever Wife wanted was fine with him. Or maybe he'd just be a really great guy and would defer the entire thing to Wife in an effort to make her happy. All within a specific budget, of course. What I didn't expect were husbands who were way too involved in the decision-making process to the point of railroading their wives, especially when they didn't really have any clue about what goes into good design, good style, good color combinations, etc. I also didn't expect husbands who picked fights with their wives over every detail and forced me to wear the hat of marriage counselor, for which I was ill-equipped. And I certainly didn't expect husbands who would pout and be obstinate just for the sake of overturning the apple cart on a design decision that Wife and I had made because he had to make his presence known at every turn. I didn't expect them to challenge me on aspects of design about which they knew little, nor did I expect them to actually belittle their wives in front of me. But that's exactly how it went down more often than not and the sole reason I made the decision to work only with single women. The husbands were simply not a pleasure to work with. Even when they started out as nice, even-tempered men, they eventually went into full-on 5-year old mode when they thought something was happening outside their control.

The beauty of being a single woman living alone is not having to deal with any of the aforementioned scenarios. You get to choose the style of your home. You get to choose the colors you want in your home. You get to choose the items that will grace your rooms, your floors, your walls. And you get to set your own budget. You won't have anyone telling you that $300 is too much to spend on a lamp. You spend that $300 if you want to and if you can afford it!

So, how do you get started designing a home for yourself that's reflective of your personality and provides a comforting haven for you to come home to? The process is actually not that different from designing a home for you and a partner. Except that you don't have to take into consideration anyone else's personal style, favorite colors, or love of Lay-Z-Boys.

IT'S ALL YOU, BABY!

The first thing to consider is how you will use each of the rooms in your home. If you have a formal dining room in addition to a kitchen eating space, but you have no earthly desire to throw a dinner party ever, then you may want to re-purpose that room as something else. A reading room? A craft room? Same goes for additional bedrooms. If you have four bedrooms and no kids, and no one ever comes to stay with you, then maybe a couple of those rooms can become a fitness room or kick-ass wine cellar. Really think about how you live, what rooms you have and what rooms you'd like to have. Just because the builder gave you a slew of bedrooms doesn't mean you have to use them as such.

Next, come up with your color scheme. Think about all the colors you love and use them liberally throughout your home. Remember, you're not pleasing anyone else here, just yourself, so you can go crazy with the colors you love. When I was in high school my family moved to a new home and my parents told me I could paint my room any color I wanted. I chose a mint green floral wallpaper accompanied by baby pink paint. Hey, it was the '80's and those colors were cool! I loved, loved, loved my room, even though my parents hated it, because it was so me! Think of your home exactly the same way. Some people are afraid to use bold color because they think their rooms will turn out looking garish. Here's how you get around that. If you love bright red or dark purple, you don't have to paint all of the walls bright red or dark purple with rugs to match.

You can go neutral with the big things, such as flooring, walls, and large pieces of furniture. Then add your bold colors in small amounts – pillows on a sofa, artwork, small rugs, a bedding pattern, drapery panels. You get to have the colors you want surrounding you without creating something that looks like an amusement park funhouse.

Then define your style. Are you a city mouse or a country mouse? Do you like rustic materials with lots of texture or sleek, clean lines? Are you traditional or modern? Casual or formal? If your head is spinning right now because you have no idea what your style is or you've never taken the time to define it, here's an easy way to get started: Get a few home magazines or go online and search interior design sites. Collect photos that you love, determine what it is about the photo that you love - overall style, color scheme, a particular furniture piece or floor tile. Make note of what you love about each photo and then see where the similarities come in between the photos. If in most of your photos you like the clean lines, grey color schemes, and use of metal and glass, then your style is likely quite urban modern. If you liked the floral patterns, soft colors and chipped-paint furniture, then your style is likely very feminine and shabby-chic. Notice what you like and don't like and try to mimic in your own rooms with what you've seen in the photos.

FINALLY, YOU WANT TO SURROUND YOURSELF WITH THINGS THAT YOU LOVE. THINGS THAT REFLECT YOUR PERSONALITY AND WHO YOU ARE.

Things from your favorite home goods store. Things that you've collected on your travels that remind you of fun times. If you don't have a favorite home goods store or haven't collected anything on your travels, what are you waiting for? Every time I'm in a cute little town with cute little shops that I've never been to before, I buy a cute little something for my home. Maybe it's a piece of artwork from a local artist. Maybe it's a tchotchke that reflects the particular town I'm in. Maybe it's just a refrigerator magnet or a Christmas ornament, but it's something that will adorn my home and remind me of the wonderful time I had on that particular trip in that particular place. It's those kinds of things that make your home unique, comforting and very YOU. Maybe you like antiques and you go antiquing wherever you are. Maybe you like the local artists in your town and you fill your home with their creations. Maybe you're just addicted to the Crate & Barrel catalog and buy all things Crate. That's okay, too. The point is to surround yourself with things you love that have meaning for you and bring you comfort.

If all of this is making you dazed and confused, and you have the money to do so, hire a professional interior designer. It's a designer's job to help you navigate all of this. They help you select things that you love. They put it all together for you so that you have a cohesive home that flows from room to room. They also ask the right questions to get at your personality and your personal style. They "get" you and what you're after. When you're single, your home should read the way your room did when you were a kid. No, you're probably not going to have a pile of stuffed animals on the bed and Madonna posters on the wall, but your home will be uniquely you, with no Lay-Z-Boy in the living room pointed directly at the TV, with food crumbs all around it. Once you have your home the way you want it, and you feel comfortable and happy in your space, you will have set the foundation for living your best life. You've heard the saying "home is where the heart is?" The reason this saying rings true for us is that your home is where you spend the majority of your down time, your "you time." You sleep there. You eat there. You bathe and dress there. You laugh there. You cry there. Your children and/or pets are there. All of your cherished belongings are there. It's your sanctuary, your haven, the place you can go to just be yourself in sweatpants with no makeup and your hair in a scrunchie. It's such an important part of your life, and in living your best life you deserve for it to be uniquely yours.

THE WORK

1. What are the things you see as good things about living alone? If you can't think of any, try taking one of your negative thoughts about living alone and turning it around. For example, if you believe that living alone means there's no one to share the household chores with, write, "The household chores get done how I want and when I want because I'm in complete control of them. Plus, the house doesn't get as messy because it's just me!"

2. Write down all of the rooms in your home and define how you would like to use them. Do you maybe want to convert your formal dining room into a craft room?

3. What are your favorite colors or the colors that you'd most like to see in your home? Remember, it's okay to use a backdrop of neutrals and throw your favorites in there as splashes of color.

4. What's your style? If you need help, refer to home magazines and the Internet.

5. Do an analysis of your home. Start with the floors, then the walls, ceilings, finishes, fixtures, furnishings, lighting, artwork and accessories. What needs to be changed? What can be changed right now and what needs to wait due to money or other constraints?

6. Write out the steps you need to take to get from point A (where you are now) to point B (where you want to be). This is your plan for getting your home in order.

CHAPTER 16

FAMILY AND FRIENDS

I n addition to our homes laying a foundation for living our best lives, our family and friends play an important part in that, as well.

WHILE LIFE DOESN'T HAVE TO BE ABOUT HAVING A RELATIONSHIP (ROMANTIC, THAT IS), LIFE IS ABOUT THE RELATIONSHIPS THAT YOU HAVE.

And if you don't have a romantic relationship then the other relationships you do have in your life play a very important role for you. Of course the love of family, friends, kids and pets isn't the same as romantic love, but why can't it be enough? You have all of the love in your life that a woman in a romantic relationship has. Instead of relying on one person for most of it, which may not actually happen anyway, you spread the responsibility over many reliable sources. All of this love can absolutely be enough for you if you also have a great love of self. If you don't love yourself then it doesn't matter how much others love you, you won't accept that as real and you won't believe that you deserve it. Let me give you a little example of what I mean.

I have a friend who dated a man for a couple of years, even asking him to move in after a few months. While there were good times during their relationship, this man treated her poorly, got her to pay all the bills even though he was working, was cold and unresponsive, said hateful things to her, and eventually dumped her out of the blue, breaking her heart. She was devastated after this man left, even though all of her friends thought it was the best thing that could've happened. She went to therapy and even got on anti-depressants to help deal with the pain of this loss. What was so sad was that this woman had three loving children, loving parents and siblings, friends who thought the world of her, and even three adoring pets. Now, all of that love didn't mean that she wouldn't feel the pain of getting her heart broken, of course, which is why she suffered despite it.

About six months later this man reappeared in her life (the craptastic ones always do) and she welcomed him back with open arms. Whaaat?! Of course all of her friends and family were appalled by this turn of events and advised her in the kindest way possible not to go down that path again. But she ignored all the advice and went forward with this man anyhow, even inviting him to move back in. I was discussing the situation with a mutual friend of ours and this friend said, "She has kids and a family who love her, isn't that enough?"

It should have been enough, but it wasn't because this woman didn't love herself. This was evident by the way she allowed this man to treat her, by how hard she took it when he left, and by the fact that after all he'd done, including bad-mouthing her to their mutual friends after he'd left, she still took him back, no questions asked. She didn't love herself and was therefore looking for that validation in another. We went over all of this in the first part of this book, so I'm not going to rehash it here, but basically she needed the perception that this man loved her in order to feel worthy. If she had had a strong love for herself then the love of her family and friends would have been enough for her and she wouldn't have allowed this horrid man back into her life.

I realized this for myself after I stopped The Endless Search and fell in love with me. All of a sudden, I started to value the love of my parents and friends more than I ever had. Just knowing that those people loved me became enough because of the intense love I had for myself. Had I not had that love for myself, I would still have been looking for it outside myself from a romantic partner and wouldn't have been able to achieve happiness on my own. That's why I talked about how important loving yourself is in the first part of this book. Once you're able to love yourself, then the loving relationships that you're in with family and friends become enough to sustain you. And you won't ever let another douchebag into your life ever again. I know it sounds cliché, but the most important love you'll ever have is the love of self.

YOU HAVE TO FALL IN LOVE WITH YOURSELF.

When you're in love with yourself you'll treat yourself well, you'll make good choices for yourself, you'll live your happiest, best life, and you'll be able to give your best to the people around you. You deserve to love yourself!

You'll also be able to recognize the best that the people around you are giving to you. You'll value it and those relationships will be all the better for it. I've never felt that my family was very close. I have a very small family and we moved around a lot when I was a kid. My parents are both only children, so I have no aunts and uncles, no cousins, and only one sibling. My entire family consisted of my parents, two sets of grandparents, and my brother. You'd think we would've been very close, but we really weren't. After my brother and I grew up and moved out of the house, we scattered and lived in separate states from my parents, our grandparents, and each other. Although we all get along just fine for the most part, we only see each other a couple times a year and don't even talk on the phone that often. After I found self-love my relationships with my parents started to grow deeper. No longer did I see them as the people who judged everything I did and didn't approve of a lot of it. No longer did I see them as authoritative and unyielding. I saw them for who they are – flawed human beings just like the rest of us. Did they change their behavior in any way? No, they're who they are. But because I love myself exactly how I am, I was able to stop thinking they were judging me or caring what they thought of me. Who were they to judge, after all? I started visiting my parents more and talking about more personal things. I was confident in myself and comfortable sharing more of myself. And a strange thing happened. I stopped thinking that they were judging everything I did and because of that shift they started supporting me more. It's hard not to support someone who so obviously loves themself. For the first time in my life I was happy with the relationship I had with my parents and I continue to value it very much.

If you're lucky enough to have a close, loving family then maybe you already appreciate and value the love that you get from them. If your family is not close, all is not lost. When you change how you feel about yourself, chances are how you feel about your family and how they feel about you will change, as well. If you don't have any family or your family is so far estranged that you feel there's no way of getting it back, then your friendships will play an even greater role in your life than maybe they do for other people. Before my breakthrough with my parents I considered my friends to be my family and even now I still do. These are the people you see and speak to on a daily basis. These are the people who know everything about you and accept you anyway (tee hee!). These are the people who choose to be in your life and choose to give you their love so it's an honor to call them friends.

If you haven't heard this expression about friendships, it's a good one.

"YOUR FRIENDS ARE GOD'S APOLOGY FOR YOUR RELATIVES."

Let's face it, no matter how good your relationship may be with your family, chances are there are still some struggles there. These generally come from the agendas we place on others that they fail to live up to and the agendas they place on us that we fail to live up to. There's less of that going on with friends. While we still likely place agendas on our friends, it's less important to us that they live up to them and our agendas are likely less rigid to begin with. If someone is not the kind of person that we'd like them to be then we probably won't make friends with them to begin with. It's much easier to cut a friend loose than it is to never speak to your mom again. So, generally speaking, your friends are made up of a group of people whom you love, who love you, you don't expect anything from each other besides you who are, and you're there for each other on life's journey, sharing the ups and downs. This is why as a single woman your friendships are so important. Because you don't have that one person in your life who shares all of this with you, your network of friendships is worth developing.

What do you do if you feel like you don't have any friends, you don't have any single friends, or your friendships could use some TLC? Friendships needing TLC is the easy one. Simply schedule more time with these people. The more time you spend with someone the closer you will get. We all lead fast-paced lives these days with little time for friendship nurturing, but nurture you must! These are your peeps and they're important to you. Try scheduling a monthly get-together that's on your calendars for a specific day every month, say the third Thursday of the month, so that it's easy for you both to stick to it. Choose an activity you both enjoy doing together and go for it. I've recently started setting up a lot of these pre-scheduled meetings with friends, otherwise six months goes by and neither of you has made a move toward getting together. I have a friend that I get together with once every other month for dinner at a nice restaurant. This not only allows us to see each other every couple of months at a minimum, but it also provides us the opportunity to try some of the many amazing restaurants in our city that we just haven't gotten around to yet.

If you're feeling that all of your friends are married and you'd like to have some single ones, I feel your pain. Back in my late 20's, my friend, Rachel, and I found ourselves the only two single girls in our friend group. That was the time when all of our friends seemed to be coupling up, getting married and starting families. Translation – they no longer wanted to get trashed with us at the bars until 2:00 AM, or no longer could, anyway. After sitting at the bar one night for the hundredth time with just the two of us staring across a bar table at each other, we decided to do something about it. This was back in the day of Yahoo Personals ads, and one evening with beers in hand the two of us huddled around my computer and wrote our ad. We were looking for single girls like us who found that all of their friends were getting married or otherwise coupling up and abandoning them, and who needed some single friends to do things with. In our entire medium-large city we got three responses. I believe we were ahead of our time and probably most people were weirded out by our ad, but we set up a happy hour meeting with those who had responded. Two of the three girls showed up and one of them was clearly uncomfortable with the situation. The other one became a friend of ours. That was short-lived when she single-white-femaled me and tried to assume my identity in a non-financial way. Needless to say, the experiment didn't work out too well, but lucky for you it's no longer the '90's and you have options.

There are Meetup groups for singles, singles activities groups, and even groups that are not specifically for singles, but that will likely have a lot of single members. Married people with kids don't have time for these groups and married people without kids have each other and probably a few couple-friends, so they're not likely to be there, either. In the past I have attended a few of these meetings, but with the hidden agenda of meeting a potential mate. I was always disappointed when I found that the majority of people at these meetings were women and of the men who were there, 90% of them were undateable. This bodes well for you, though, because single girlfriends is what you're after. Aside from specific group get-togethers, it's important for the single woman seeking single girlfriends to say yes to lots of activities. Say yes to that party invitation even though you'll know only the host. Say yes to that hiking club you've had your eye on.

SAY YES TO ANY OPPORTUNITY THAT PUTS YOU WITH PEOPLE YOU DON'T ALREADY KNOW. YOU HAVE NO IDEA WHO YOU'RE LIKELY TO MEET AND NOTHING TO LOSE.

I'm a wine drinker and I recently researched wine clubs in my area online. I found only one and it was a wine dinner-style club that met once a month. I knew absolutely no one there, but decided to go to my first event anyway. If nothing else I could focus on my food and the wine presentation. I spent the social hour part of the evening keeping to myself and sampling as many wines as I could, but after I made a comment to a woman standing next to me about one of the wines, we struck up a conversation and she invited me to sit at her table with two of her other single friends. Jackpot! I became fast friends with the other two ladies and we've been friends for over a year now. It was as easy as that. Single women are everywhere. We attend events in droves, especially anything where wine is being served. We have multiple interests and we love going out together. When a single male friend of mine said to me one day, "I don't know where to meet single women," I exclaimed, "Are you kidding me? We're everywhere! Just go to any event that's not a monster truck rally and we'll be all over the place."

The same principles apply to you single girls who feel that you don't have any friends at all, single or otherwise. Chances are you actually do have some friends and maybe those friendships just need to be nurtured, as we talked about earlier in this chapter. If you need to expand your network, and by all means you should, then get yourself out there. Don't be afraid to say yes to things. Don't be afraid to attend events by yourself. Even if you're an introvert, someone like me will likely start talking to you. Attend events that interest you and at least you'll get the benefit of some education or an experience, if you don't happen to meet your future BFF there. And then when you do meet someone you'd like to be friends with, put forth a little effort. You don't need to stalk the person, but make a move to try to get together with them. So many people I know who claim to not have many friends aren't bothering to put any effort into finding and developing those friendships.

LIKE ANY RELATIONSHIP, FRIENDSHIPS TAKE WORK.

If you're looking for the kind of friendship that doesn't take any work, may I recommend adopting a pet?

I actually wasn't joking about that. Well, maybe about the no-work part, but not about adopting a pet. I can't talk about friends and family without including pets in the mix. If you haven't gotten it yet from the rest of this book, I'm a cat person. Really, I'm just an animal person, period. I think animals enrich our lives in ways we probably don't even recognize. I have two cats and as far I'm concerned they're my kids, especially since I don't have any actual kids. I know you've heard this before, but animals give us unconditional love. Unconditional love! What other love on earth is unconditional? Even the love you have for yourself is probably not completely unconditional. Yet a cat will still love you even after you pin him down and trim his claws. And a dog will lovingly lick your face even after you've cooped her up in a crate for nine hours. Animals can certainly fill a love void if you happen to be experiencing one in your life.

Animals will greet you at the door when you come home, excited to see you. They'll curl up in your lap especially when you need them the most. They'll sleep in your bed with you and remind you that you're not alone. They'll do whacky things that make you laugh every day. They'll put their faces in your face and share a moment with you. They'll get you up out of bed and maybe even out the door. They'll go for a car ride with you. They'll share your meal with you, whether you want them to or not. They'll alert you and protect you. They'll be there for you always. They have no choice, you're holding them captive. Sure, they'll also throw up on your favorite rug, eat your favorite plant and chew up your Manolos, but that's proof positive that ALL relationships take work.

I often run across single people who have no pets. Sometimes there are allergies or a lot of travel for work or something like that that keeps them from having a pet, but when those variables are absent I really can't believe that they don't have a pet. I once had both of my cats pass away within two months of each other. I was devastated and knew it was going to be some time before I was able to adopt another cat. But when I would leave the house there was no one to say goodbye to and when I would return home there was no one to greet me at the door and demand dinner. My house was so empty and so quiet, and it just didn't feel like home! It took about one month before I realized that I needed to adopt a couple of cats, and when I did I fell in love with them immediately.

PETS HAVE THE POWER TO TURN YOUR FOUL MOOD AROUND AND TO MAKE YOU SMILE IN SPITE OF YOURSELF. THEY ALSO HAVE THE POWER TO GIVE YOU SOMETHING TO LIVE FOR OUTSIDE OF YOURSELF.

After losing a job that I had had for eight years, I fell into a depression that was deeper than anything I had ever experienced. The economy was bad and I wasn't finding a new job. Unemployment compensation didn't cover the bills and I watched my savings dwindle to nothing as the months passed by. I sold all of the stock I owned and even had to borrow some money from my parents just to pay the bills. I couldn't even get on the phone with them without bursting into tears at some point during the conversation. I had no idea when I was going to get a job, what type of job it would be, or if it would pay enough to keep me afloat. I wondered if I would lose my home and if I did what I would do. I walked around with a little grey cloud over my head each and every day. I couldn't get my situation off my mind long enough to even enjoy a movie or a walk around the lake. I was in such deep despair that I made a decision one day. I decided that if it all got to be too much, I had a choice. I didn't have to deal with it anymore. I could go. You understand what I mean by "go," right? I'm not talking about selling everything I owned and moving to South America to sell toe rings on the beach. I didn't make any plans or start researching any methods or anything like that, but I gave myself the option. I mentally went through the list of my family and friends and determined how my actions might affect their lives. I decided that they would all be sad, but they would all be okay without me. Then I looked at my cats. And I knew there was no way in hell that I could do that to them. What would happen to them? Where would they go? Who would care for them? What if they ended up in some unpleasant situation? And how would they ever understand what happened? They wouldn't. Right then and there I stopped that train of thought. There were two living beings who needed me and I wasn't about to shirk that responsibility. Thankfully, not long after that I got a job, a good one, and things got back to normal. I still think back on that time in my life and realize how powerful the relationship between people and their pets can be, especially single people and their pets.

When you're single, your friends and family (including pets) are everything to you. They're your support system. They're the ones you tell everything to. They're the ones you laugh with and cry with. They're the ones you share all of life's ups and downs with. They're the ones who help you out when you're in a jam and celebrate all of your successes with you. They hold your hair when you puke and they fist bump you when you sink a 30-foot putt. Tell your friends, family and pets that you love them. Tell them all the time. And make those that can speak say it back. This is the one time where this is okay. I want to end this chapter by getting all sappy on your asses and thanking the many wonderful friends I've had over the years who've loved me, helped me, supported me, and who I never would've made it through this single life without:

SHERRI (MY BFF): Thank you for going to the nude beach on Maui with me. Thank God we did that in our 30's!

RACHEL: Thank you for throwing up on your pants at my Halloween party, then sliding down my stairs on your butt, smearing a red wine stain all down the wall of the stairwell. It was right after that we became friends, wasn't it?

ALEX: Thank you for sharting in your pants at work and doing the walk of shame to Target to get a new pair. And thanks to Eric for telling me about it!

AUDREY: Thank you for saying "shit" in front of my parents when we were teenagers. It gives us something to laugh about for the rest of our lives.

KAREN: Thank you for telling me the story of when you tripped and fell getting off the elevator in Vegas while dressed up as an old lady, and the vibrator you were selling spilled onto the floor and started dancing around, much to the shock and horror of the people still on the elevator. Best story ever!

COURT: Thank you for asking me to flash you my boobs and then telling me you were "on the fence" afterward. (Court's gay, BTW)

ELDON: Thank you for always being willing to make fun of Court with me. (Eldon, also gay)

KATHY: Thank you for singing "Bust A Move" karaoke with me at that dive bar on the Oregon coast and twerking for the audience while I smacked your ass.

KEITH: Thank you for letting me call you "old man" and "old fart" even though you can kick my ass at a 5K.

ELLEN: Thank you for calling Keith "old man" and "old fart" with me, even though you're married to him. Or maybe because you're married to him?

ALL THE CATS I'VE EVER HAD: Thank you for throwing up on the arm of the sofa so that some of it dribbled down the arm onto the cushion and into the crack between the arm and cushion, and some of it dribbled down the side of the sofa and onto the carpet. The cleaning challenge was just what I needed at the time!

Okay, that did not get all sappy on your asses, did it? Let's try again, just in case you think friends are only there for entertainment value.

SHERRI: Thank you for being my BFF, for always "getting" me, and for spending hours on the phone with me when some idiot Frog had broken my heart.

RACHEL: Thank you for your loyal friendship even when I was being less than loyal, and for navigating our 20's and 30's with me.

ALEX: Thank you for listening to me whine about my weight, money and everything else, and for commiserating with me. You're a good person!

AUDREY: Thank you for reaching out to me when I really needed someone and for picking up where we left off after 10 years of not seeing/speaking to each other.

KAREN: Thank you for your always-compassionate heart and words of wisdom.

COURT: Thank you for always telling me I'm hot, even at times when we both know I'm not.

ELDON: Thank you for helping me through a difficult time and not judging my feelings.

KATHY: Thank you for being so much like me that if we weren't both hetero girls we probably would've gotten married and lived happily ever after.

KEITH: Thank you for always being there for me when I've gotten into jams and always being willing to drop everything to help me out of them.

ELLEN: Thank you for lending me your husband so that I have someone to call when I get into jams and need help out of them.

ALL THE CATS I'VE EVER HAD: Thank you for making me laugh every single day, loving me unconditionally and allowing me to do the same, and saving my life in ways you could never know.

AND THAT'S WHY FRIENDS AND FAMILY (AND PETS!) ARE SO DANG IMPORTANT FOR THE SINGLE GIRL!

THE WORK

1. What familial relationships do you value the most? Write down the family members who mean the most to you and why. What can you do to enrich these relationships?

2. What friendships do you value the most? Write down the friends who mean the most to you and why. What can you do to enrich these relationships?

3. What can you do to meet new friends? Activities? Groups? Education?

4. Can you adopt a pet? What type of pet will you adopt?

5. Write out the steps you need to take to get from point A (where you are now) to point B (where you want to be). This is your plan for getting your family and friend relationships in order.

CHAPTER 17

HEALTH AND FITNESS

W e can't talk about creating a plan for you to live your best life without talking about your health. Health and fitness lay the groundwork for every day to be a happy day. In fact, I've heard many self-help gurus say that you can't make all of the good things happen in your life if you're neglecting your health and fitness. I'm not sure I completely agree with this, but it's definitely part of the total package. Being healthy and fit seems to make everything else in life easier, even bending down to tie your shoe. And who doesn't want living the single-girl life to be easier? That's why you picked up this book, right?

Before we get into the meat of this chapter I want to state for the record that I am not a health professional. Nor am I a fitness trainer or nutritionist of any kind. Anything I share about health, fitness or nutrition is based on personal experience, and commonly accepted beliefs and practices.

For the past several months I've been practicing a health and fitness program of my own design that has profoundly affected my well-being, including my mood, energy level and confidence. It hasn't always been this way. I've gained and lost hundreds of pounds over the years and have gone from practicing near-vegetarianism to eating McDonald's three times a week and back again. I've gone from running a half marathon to not even being able to run a half mile. I've let the devastation from breakups render me incapable of exercise and have instead sought solace in a pepperoni pizza with extra cheese. I've chosen food to comfort me during the difficult times because I felt I had no one to turn to. I've let the fact that I don't "have anyone" in my life produce a why-bother attitude since there's no one to be healthy and fit for. But just like every other aspect of our single-girl lives, WE are the ones that we need to be healthy and fit for.

Let's start by talking about actual health problems outside of just regular everyday eating and exercise issues. If you have any health problems, especially ones that keep you from being able to exercise, then now is the time to get on top of them. Go see your doctor and get on a plan to tackle these health problems. It may require medication or surgery or a change in diet, but whatever it takes, these things don't usually get better on their own and they don't do you any good when you're trying to get your life in order. A friend of mine's wife died of breast cancer many years ago. It was a long, painful battle and what he said was most profound about the experience was that when your health or someone you love's health is in jeopardy, nothing else in life matters during that time. Not your job or your home or your friends or anything else. All that matters is that health problem and you're powerless to tend to anything else in your life. So, do yourself a favor and take the steps you need to get your health problems under control. Your life will thank you.

Assuming you don't have any major health issues and you're basically healthy, then it's diet and exercise that you really need to focus on.

IT SEEMS LIKE EVERY TIME I READ SOMETHING ABOUT ANY PROBLEM IN LIFE, THE SOLUTION IS ALWAYS TO EAT RIGHT AND EXERCISE.

Don't have any energy during the day? Eat more fruits and vegetables and get regular exercise. Down in the dumps more often than you'd like? Eat more fruits and vegetables and get regular exercise. Your BFF is moving to Zimbabwe? Set up a Skype account. Oh, and eat more fruits and vegetables and get regular exercise. I even love the myriad of weight loss product ads that go on and on about how skinny they're going to make you, and then at the very end they tell you that they work in combination with a healthy diet and exercise. Maybe just try the healthy diet and exercise and see how far that gets you?

If you're a yo-yo dieting single girl like I am, here's how your adult life has probably gone. You start dating someone new and exciting, and you immediately lose 20 lbs because you forget to eat while your head is filled only with thoughts of him, not of actual meals. As you settle into the relationship your rate of weight loss starts to slow down, especially when you realize that he wants to see you naked whether your thighs are perfect or not. You also spend a lot of time going out to eat together, but not a whole lot of time working out together, except in the bedroom. Your weight loss stagnates and you may even put on a few pounds from all the eating out coupled with how comfortable you are with the love of your life. Then the relationship starts to sour a little and your clothes start to get a little tighter. By the time you break up you've put back on that 20 lbs, plus 10 more. And now for the post-breakup depression, characterized by tubs of ice cream in the freezer and your Chipotle rewards card getting more of a workout than you do. Here comes 20 more lbs! Now you're fat and alone and no one loves you, except the people at the Dunkin' Donuts drive-thru. Do we see the vicious cycle here? When we're single it's easy to "let ourselves go," so to speak, because there's no one else looking at us and picturing us in a thong. This type of thinking does not go along with the loving-yourself-and-living-for-yourself premise of this book, however, so I'm going to show you how to get out of this thinking and start living a healthy lifestyle for you and only you.

First of all, everyone needs to eat a healthy diet and exercise regularly. Everyone. It's the cornerstone of good health.

EVEN PEOPLE WHO DON'T NEED TO LOSE WEIGHT STILL NEED TO EAT A HEALTHY DIET AND EXERCISE REGULARLY.

I know people who are overweight and are in better health than their skinny counterparts because they eat healthy and exercise instead of relying on their absurdly high metabolism while wolfing down a burger and fries. If you need to lose weight then focusing on your diet and exercise plan is even more important for you, but even if your weight is healthy you still need to take a look at what you're putting into your body on a daily basis and how much you move.

Rather than talk about specifically what to eat or how much, I'm going to be a bit more general. Everyone is different. Everyone has different calorie needs. Everyone likes different things. Everyone believes different research about what is the healthiest way to eat. Some people believe in a low fat diet. Some people consume no animal products. Some people believe that cutting out carbs is the key. I think these people are crazy, but what do I know? I'll tell you what I know: everyone must interpret the vast array of nutrition research out there the best they can and find something that works for them. I took a nutrition class in college and there was a textbook that went along with it. The author of this textbook proclaimed that the healthiest way to eat was unprocessed, whole foods in a certain balance. Your plate was supposed to contain half fruits and veggies, a quarter protein and a quarter carbs. Is any of this sounding familiar? It was over 30 years ago that this textbook was written, but the premise of the book is the same one that the plant-based proponents use today. And the plant-based movement is on the rise to take over the meat-based movement.

Whichever plan you decide to follow, it needs to be something that you can do long-term. Eating lots of meat and no carbs is probably not sustainable and is likely not that healthy. Eating very little fat and lots of refined carbs falls into the same category. Some basic principles apply no matter what. Meat should be lean, carbs should be whole grain, dairy should be low-fat, and plant-based fats are good for you in moderation. Sugar from fruit is also good for you in moderation, but refined sugar doesn't do you any good and should be limited. Alcohol is good in moderation, too. Salt should be limited. Vegetables are the superstars of nutrition ass-kickery. I think most people out there would agree with these statements, but if you don't then that's okay, too.

THE KEY IS THAT YOU DO THE BEST YOU CAN AND FIND SOMETHING THAT WORKS FOR YOU LONG-TERM.

Why does it need to work long-term? Why can't you just go on a high protein diet, lose some weight, and then go back to eating the way you are now? Because if you've ever tried this, or any other diet for that matter, this approach doesn't work. You lose weight because you're cutting calories and you've increased your metabolism with exercise, but as soon as you go back to consuming the amount of calories you consume now and you stop exercising, all that weight is going to creep back on. It's much easier to find something that you can do for the rest of your life and just start living that way without having to put much thought into it ever again. And if you don't need to lose weight, but just need to healthen up, then this applies to you specifically. You need to choose a plan that's sustainable for you, and that you're going to be happy with for the rest of your life. How do you do this?

I call it "thinking from the end," which I learned from one of my favorite self-development gurus, the late Dr. Wayne Dyer. Dr. Dyer talked about imagining your life as already being the way you'd like it to be and behaving as if it's already so. He follows it up with the practice of affirmations where you actually tell yourself on a daily basis, "I am a healthy, fit, size 6," or whatever. While he didn't specifically apply this principle to weight loss or fitness, he did mean for it to apply to all aspects of life, so this would be included. I decided to apply it to health and fitness and here's what I came up with: I imagined the Universe coming to me with her magic wand (cuz the Universe is a woman and she has a magic wand, y'know), and waving that wand over me and making me my ideal weight and fitness level. Then the Universe says to me, "Okay, I gave you what you wanted, now you have to figure out how to maintain it. I ain't gonna do that part for you!" So, how would I maintain it? This is where the plan comes in.

Would I be willing to eat only 1,000 calories and work out for three hours a day? No. Would I be willing to never eat a donut or piece of cheesecake ever again? No. Would I be willing to give up wine for the rest of my life? Hells no! So, what would I be willing to do? Would I be willing to eat healthy most of the time, with the occasional trip to McDonald's or pigout at happy hour? Yes. Would I be willing to work out for 30-60 minutes a day, six times a week? Yes. I looked at how I would function if I was already the weight/ size/shape I wanted to be and all I had to do was maintain my health. You're really not going to do more than that long-term, are you? There's only just so much exercise you're willing to do and just so little you're willing to eat. Be realistic, remember it's about your health, and put a plan together for yourself. If you're lucky enough to be in a position where you already are at the weight and size you want to be, you still need to put together a plan for yourself. Just because you don't need to lose weight doesn't mean you don't need to be healthy. You still need to exercise and eat right to support your overall health. And just because you're at a healthy weight doesn't mean you're necessarily fit, either. Exercise does this for you. You need to take a look at starting a workout regimen or increasing the intensity of your existing workouts. Exercise, just like eating, is about health, not weight.

If you need to lose weight then there's one more thing you need to do after you've put together an eating and exercise plan for yourself. I'm going to ask you to change your thinking (imagine that!) about your healthy eating and exercise plan.

AS I JUST SAID, EATING RIGHT AND EXERCISE ARE ABOUT YOUR HEALTH, NOT YOUR WEIGHT, EVEN IF YOU NEED TO LOSE WEIGHT.

You are not executing your plan with the intent of losing weight, you're executing your plan with the intent of being healthy. The weight loss will come as a delightful bonus. So, put the scale away and just focus on your health. Did I stick to my plan and eat healthy today? Were my portion sizes adequate, meaning neither too small nor too large? Did I work out for at least 30 minutes today? If you answer yes to these questions then that's your gauge of how well you're doing, not the scale. It's okay to weigh yourself when you first start down your path of healthy living and it's okay to check in every couple weeks to a month to see how much progress you're making, but being glued to the scale every day is not something that's going to help you.

Another thing to remember as you're putting your healthy eating and exercise plan together for yourself is that you have to actually like what you're eating and you have to enjoy what you're doing for your workouts. If you hate chicken breasts and broccoli then don't eat chicken breasts and broccoli, no matter how healthy you think they are. Find the healthy foods that you do like and eat those. When you plan out your meals for the week (yes, you should do this once a week so that you have a plan to stick to), make sure everything on your plan is something you're excited to eat. You'd be surprised how many healthy foods there are that you actually enjoy eating just as much as fried chicken and mashed potatoes smothered in gravy. Same goes for the exercise. If the thought of running makes you want to put a bullet in your own head, then don't run! Seems like a no-brainer, but people will do what they think is good for them regardless of how much they hate it, and how long do you think that will last? If you like to walk, then walk. If you like to ride your bike, then do that. It doesn't really matter what you do for exercise as long as you get your heart rate up there and give your muscles something to be proud of.

Just like any change, your new eating and exercise plan is not going to be super easy at first. You're going to crave all of the things you think you can't have, but remember this, you can have them. You can have them any time you want. Does a normal, healthy person never eat a donut? No. Does a normal, healthy person never skip a workout? No. Do normal, healthy people go on vacation and pig out for an entire week and regret the 5 lbs they gained just like everyone else? Yes. The difference is they go right back to their healthy eating and exercise plan, and a couple weeks later that 5 lbs is gone. Why? Because they went back to normal.

YOU'RE NOW IN THE PROCESS OF CREATING YOUR NEW NORMAL FOR EATING AND EXERCISE.

After a few weeks you'll get used to your plan and it will become second nature. You can even plan in your slips if you want. If you know you're going to happy hour with the girls on Wednesday and you'll be ordering cheese sticks and potato skins, then plan for that. One night of cheese sticks and potato skins is not going to ruin your health. Just get right back on your healthy eating plan the next morning for breakfast, do your workout the next day, and fugget about it. And for God's sake, don't weigh yourself!

I've been following this plan for several months now and it's working like a charm. I feel great physically, my mood has improved tenfold, I have the energy to do what I want, and goshdarnit, I'm proud of myself, too. I've also lost a significant amount of weight, not that that matters, right? I look at every segment of every day individually – breakfast, lunch, dinner, snack, workout – and "messing up" during one segment, such as being too lazy to haul my cookies out of bed and get on the treadmill, has no effect on the rest of the segments for that day. So, I didn't work out today, big rip. I can still eat right all day and work out extra hard tomorrow. And the farther along I get with my plan the easier it is to stick with it. I'm not gonna lie, I once spent about a year going to McDonald's for lunch 1-2 times per week, in addition to other poor eating habits. A little embarrassing, but I did it and it's over. I don't even think about going to McDonald's anymore. I've gotten so used to following my plan that I drive right past Mickey D's and onto Wendy's for a salad. In the past three months I think I've been to McD's twice and both times were planned. I mean, you still gotta live, right? So, c'mon brave single girl, make a healthy eating and exercise plan for yourself, execute it for yourself, do it for your health, give yourself some flexibility, and be proud of yourself when you not only feel great every day, but those formerly skin-tight jeans all of a sudden fit!

THE WORK

1. What health problems, if any, do you need to tackle?

2. What and how much do you eat on a daily basis? Is there room for improvement? What can you add or subtract? Remember, you need to like the food you're putting into your body and create an eating plan that you'll be able to stick with long-term.

3. How often and at what intensity do you work out? Is there room for improvement? Just like food, exercise needs to be something you enjoy doing and will stick with long-term.

4. How will you start to think about healthy eating and exercise as something you're doing for your health and not for the purpose of weight loss alone?

5. Write out the steps you need to take to get from point A (where you are now) to point B (where you want to be). This is your plan for getting your health and fitness in order.

CHAPTER 18

ACTIVITIES

I know we've been focusing on ourselves this entire book, but this is the chapter in which we get to focus on the fun part of being ourselves. In other words, we've dealt with career, home, friends and family, and health and fitness, but what about the truly fun stuff? What about hiking and baking and gardening and travel and food and wine? And Netflix? What about all the stuff that makes life fun and worth living? Sure, our relationships with other people can make life fun and worth living, but what about all the things we like to do in our free time that make us uniquely who we are? For so many of us, these activities have been determined for us by someone else. When we were children they tended to be defined by our parents and families. Whatever our families did we tended to do. As we got older we started to branch out and discover other things that interested us. Maybe a friend taught us how to ski or a teacher introduced us to the joy of reading the classics. Then we started dating and a lot of us let our activities be defined by that relationship. Let's face it, even if someone else's activities are not being forced upon you or you're not claiming someone else's recreational identity as your own, a relationship works much better when the two people involved like to do a majority of the same things. So, you tend to do those things a lot and spend less time branching out on your own. As a savvy single girl, you get to decide what, where, when and how, and you don't need anyone else in order to do the things you like to do.

Since you've given up The Endless Search you no longer need to evaluate an activity based on its likelihood to attract single men, whom you then hope to attract. I recently overheard a woman being invited to an event. There appeared to be some discussion about said event and then the woman finally said with dismay, "But how am I going to meet a man there?" Is that what determines what events you'll attend? Whether or not you'll be able to meet a man? If so then you're likely missing out on a lot of fun, friends, and wonderful experiences. Attend events because you're interested in them, because you want to enrich your friendships and meet new friends, because they give back to the community, and because they sound like FUN! Not because there may be the potential to meet a man there.

What is it you like to do? Do you spend a significant amount of your free time doing these things or do you sit at home because you think you have no one to do things with? Chances are you spend at least some of your free time doing at least some of the things you like to do and you probably keep those things going pretty well. What about the things you'd like to do that you're not currently doing? I invite you to make a list of the things you like to do that you're currently doing and another list of things you'd like to do that you are not currently doing. Then list the reasons you're not currently doing those things. Do you dream of traveling the world, but you can never find anyone to travel with and you're scared to do it alone? Or maybe you think that traveling alone will be boring or sad (or dangerous!) because you have no one to share it with? Are you interested in honing your cooking skills, but think there's no point in cooking for one? Or are you keeping yourself from trying that new activity because you don't know anyone else who does it and you don't know how to get started?

YOU DON'T WANT TO GET TO THE END OF YOUR LIFE WITH A BUCKET LIST FULL OF UNFULFILLED ACTIVITIES BECAUSE YOU WAITED AROUND FOR SOMEONE TO DO THEM WITH AND THAT PERSON NEVER CAME ALONG.

The best way to get started with a new activity is to take a class or get involved with a group who does that activity. Want to learn to rock climb? Take a class at your local gym's climbing wall. Want to start hiking? Find a hiking group that plans hikes a couple times a week. Want to learn to roll sushi? Take a class at your local cooking school. For any activity in which you're interested, there's a class or group out there, or both. I learned to scuba dive because friends of mine were going on a trip to Mexico and I was the only one who wasn't certified. After that trip I wanted to keep diving, but my dive friends had other plans, so that's when I signed up for that group trip where I made so many new friends who became an important part of my life.

I realize that finding classes and groups is more difficult if you live in a smaller community. I live in a larger city and have most everything available to me, so it's easier. If you live in a smaller town, you may just have to focus your list on those things that are more readily available to you or you may have to travel a bit to find what you're looking for. If I were to move to a small town I would find the nearest dive shop and book trips with them, even if that shop were 200 miles away. All I would have to do is drive that 200 miles on the day of the trip and meet up with the rest of the group at the airport. If there's a strong desire to do something, then there's a way to get it done. Especially with the advent of the Internet. You can connect to a group of like-minded people anywhere now. Your singleness shouldn't be a detriment to doing these things, it should actually be an asset. You won't have anyone else holding you back because they're not interested in your activity of choice. You won't have anyone saying that you can't spend money on dive equipment because diving is silly. You won't have anyone refusing to drive 200 miles to the airport to meet up with the dive group. You get to do what you want, everything that you want, and the only person that can hold you back is you.

Since we've touched on solo travel a bit, I wanted to talk about this in further detail. This is a tough one for a lot of single women. You want to travel, but you don't want to do it alone. And the reason you don't want to do it alone is because you're scared, or you think it will be boring or depressing on your own, or you think it'll be downright dangerous. But you can't find anyone with the time/money/desire to go with you. Now you're stuck in a conundrum.

DO YOU SUCK IT UP AND GO ON YOUR OWN OR DO YOU STAY HOME AND VIEW PHOTOS ON THE INTERNET OF THE PLACES YOU'D LIKE TO GO?

There are actually ways to go to all the places you'd like to go and you don't have to do it alone. If you have kids then you have built-in travel companions and you'll be enriching their lives as well as your own. Sure, you may have to go to Disney instead of Club Med, but you can save Club Med for later. In the absence of kids and friends as travel partners, there are many single-girl travel groups out there who go on trips all over the world. I know a couple women who swear by these groups, have done multiple trips with them, and have seen half the world. You may have to get yourself to a certain city to meet up with the group, but after that all of your arrangements are made for you and there's safety in numbers. You may even meet some women who become lifelong friends.

If group travel is not for you, but you're still leery of going it alone, why not start small? Book a weekend for yourself in the cute little wine town a few hours' drive away. Research places to stay that are near the action so that restaurants and activities are close, and plan out your agenda for the entire time you're there so that you don't have hours of alone time with nothing do except lament the fact that you're alone. Do all of the things that YOU want to do when YOU want to do them. Once you've done this and seen how much fun you can have on your own, you'll be ready to graduate to flying somewhere and renting a car. Then maybe flying to another country. There are also many solo travel sites out there to help you with the details, and give you safety tips pertaining to where to stay and places to avoid where you may get your cell phone stolen by a guy on a bike. The point is to start somewhere. Like with all things, the more you do something the easier it gets and the more you start to enjoy it. Bon voyage!

We also touched on cooking and the single girl, which I know is a tough one for a lot of you, so I wanted to go into that in further detail, as well. For many years I was in the "why bother" camp of cooking for one. Then my desire to actually chop vegetables in my kitchen and eat something that didn't come out of a package won out. I started to cook for myself and my life got exponentially better. Cooking for yourself is healthier and less expensive than eating out or buying pre-prepared foods all the time. And it sure as hell beats eating popcorn over the sink!

IT'S WORTH THE EFFORT TO MAKE HEALTHY, DELICIOUS MEALS FOR YOURSELF BECAUSE TAKING CARE OF YOURSELF IS JUST AS IMPORTANT AS TAKING CARE OF A SIGNIFICANT OTHER OR A FAMILY.

Think of it this way, for the married woman and/or married with kids, cooking can become a chore, something they have to do because they have to take care of others. For you, lucky single girl, it's something you GET to do. You get to cook what you want when you want, too. No chicken fingers and tater tots for you, you get baked Alaskan salmon with balsamic glaze, sautéed green beans almondine, Dijon-roasted potatoes, and flourless chocolate torte for dessert.

Where do you start if you're interested in cooking for yourself, but you don't know the first thing about cooking? Well, of course there are classes you can take at your local culinary shop or your community college's continuing education program. Not to mention the wealth of online tutorials available today. Personally, I started with the good ol' Food Network. Find a chef you like whose dishes seem simple to prepare and watch what they do. You'll start to learn food lingo, what all those gadgets are for and how to use them, and what in the world nutritional yeast is. You can download the recipes you like and give it a whirl. The more you cook for yourself the better you'll get at it. When I first started I followed the recipes to a T. There's nothing wrong with doing that. As time goes by you'll find you're substituting ingredients to tailor the recipe more to your liking or make it healthier. Of course, most recipes are written for at least four servings and you won't need that much unless you truly love leftovers, but you can easily cut them down to two servings. Bon appetit!

YOUR HAPPINESS AS A SINGLE WOMAN DEPENDS LARGELY ON YOUR ABILITY TO ENJOY YOUR OWN COMPANY AND ENJOYING YOUR OWN COMPANY IS A SKILL THAT REQUIRES PRACTICE.

Doing the things that you love to do on your own makes your alone time much more enjoyable than does sitting on the couch rolled up in a ball under your blankie thinking about how lonely you are. For most of the activities any of us is looking to do, you don't need another person to do them with you, you just need the strength to do them on your own and trust me, single girl, you've got the strength. Which is worse – feeling a little awkward going to the movies by yourself or missing that blockbuster hit that everyone's talking about? Struggling to change your flattened bike tire on the trail by yourself or missing out on that incredible mountain view? Booking that solo trip to Italy where the only words you know are spaghetti, ravioli and gelato or living out your life listening to other people's stories of their trips there? In order to be who you really want to be and live your best life, you've got to do the things that you really want to do. There's no time like the present to get started. Make your list and get moving!

THE WORK

1. What recreational activities do you currently engage in?

2. What additional activities would you like to add to this list? And which ones from the list would you like to do more often?

3. Are there certain activities that you don't wish to do alone or which actually require another person? What groups can you join so that you have people to do these things with?

4. Do you currently cook for yourself? Would you like to? What do you need to learn or equip yourself with in order to start doing this?

5. Write out the steps you need to take to get from point A (where you are now) to point B (where you want to be). This is your plan for getting your activities in order.

CHAPTER 19

COMMUNITY

The final aspect of your life that you need to get in shape so that you can live your best single-girl life is Community. Community can mean a lot of things. It doesn't necessarily have anything to do with the geographic area in which you live, but it can. For our purposes here, I'm going to talk about community in two ways: 1. Your personal relationships outside of friends and family, and 2. Your impact on the world. Community is where you both connect with others and give back. As single women we have the opportunity to be highly involved in our communities. Since we're not tending to romantic relationships and may not be tending to children, either, it leaves us with some extra time to engage in community and some extra heart to share with others. Now, if you're a single girl who's working 80 hours a week then having extra time to be present in your community may not be an option for you. If you're caring for children you may not have much extra time, either. For those of you with time on your hands, giving back and engaging with others outside of your friends and family can have a profound effect on how you feel about the life you're leading. I'm talking about using your singleness to your advantage and the advantage of others. Using your extra time to connect with lots of other people and your extra energy for doing something good. Like when people take something profound that has happened to them, such as winning the lottery, and use it to start a foundation or something instead of just blowing it all on a ticket for a flight to the moon.

CONNECTING WITH PEOPLE OUTSIDE OF YOUR FRIENDS AND FAMILY IS IMPORTANT FOR THE SINGLE GIRL BECAUSE IT BROADENS YOUR CIRCLE AND FILLS UP THE SPACE IN YOUR HEART THAT YOU HAVE AVAILABLE FOR OTHERS.

While friends and family are likely the closest to you and the most important to you, there are also coworkers, classmates, neighbors, the people with whom you volunteer down at the soup kitchen, and the ladies on your softball team. There are people everywhere, which is why there's no way anyone can consider themselves alone unless you've chosen to exile yourself to a tiny cabin in the wilderness of Alaska. Even then you probably have at least grizzly bears and caribou to keep you company. But assuming you live in a regular city or town, you have people all around you. Not to mention all the social media channels you can use to connect to others, as well as the fact that your network of peeps can get a hold of you via multiple communication channels at any time of the day or night. I find myself having a harder time getting some time to myself than I do finding people to do things with and activities to participate in. And I'm grateful for this! It's much easier to stop lamenting the fact that you don't have a mate when you have all of these other people who like you, care about you, and depend on you.

Connecting with others can come in many shapes and sizes. It can include some of the activities you enjoy that you defined for yourself in the last chapter. If you like to play golf, why not join a ladies golf league and connect with fellow golfers in your area. If you like to cook, take some group cooking classes and start a "supper club" with the other students that you meet. If you like to read, start a book club and post it on social media or on the bulletin board at your local bookstore for others to join. There are so many ways to connect with others on a personal level and build your circle of human connections even if you never end up becoming besties with any of these people. I have people with whom I play golf and nothing else, but we enjoy each other's company on the course and in the clubhouse afterward for lunch. I have people whom I see only once a year on our annual group scuba diving trip, but we have a blast together for an entire week and I include them in my social circle. Your circle can and should include lots of people you like, even if you are not especially close to all of them.

WAYS TO MEET PEOPLE AND CONNECT WITH OTHERS:

- Take a class in something you're interested in, like learning to speak Italian, then form a group of your classmates who get together to practice ordering pizza and limoncello.

- Attend your neighborhood picnic and get to know your neighbors, then organize a progressive dinner. At their houses.
- Join a golf league, tennis league, volleyball league, fencing league, dodge ball league. Go for drinks afterward.
- Attend seminars and actually talk to the people around you.
- Volunteer for a cause in which you believe and bake vegan cupcakes for their annual bake sale. Yep, they exist.
- Find a travel group and when you meet people you like find out what other upcoming trips they're going on and sign up for the same ones. No, this is not considered stalking, it's connecting!

There are so many ways to expand your circle and you never know, you may just end up making a new acquaintance or two who become close personal friends. Just having all of these activities in which you're involved and where you interact with other like-minded people gives you an amazing sense of community and belonging. It's also good for the soul to have others who depend on you for things. While that may seem like something that adds to your stress level and piles even more responsibility on your plate, it also gives you the chance to be needed. We all need to be needed to some level. Significant others need us. Children need us. In the absence of those people, who needs you? Your extended circle needs you, that's who. So take something you really like to do, or something you want to learn, or something you truly believe in and then figure out a way to do it while interacting with others. And if you can find a way to give back while connecting with others, all the better.

Community goes way beyond just doing fun things that make you happy and meeting others in the process.

BELIEVE IT OR NOT, THERE'S NOTHING MORE FULFILLING THAN DOING SOMETHING THAT BENEFITS SOMEONE ELSE JUST OUT OF THE GOODNESS OF YOUR HEART WHILE NOT EXPECTING ANYTHING IN RETURN.

I'm talking about giving back to your community through volunteerism. This doesn't even have to mean a formal charitable organization or a regular commitment. You could mow your elderly neighbor's lawn while she's laid up after a knee replacement. Or bake cookies for your friend's child's class because you know she doesn't have time. There are so many little things you can do for others that will warm both their heart and yours. And if you do desire to volunteer with a formal organization there are many, many of those that need your help.

If you don't know specifically which organization or type of organization you'd like to volunteer with, think about your interests. Do you love animals and also the outdoors? Volunteer with your local shelter or rescue group to take the dogs on long walks, runs or hikes. Do you love working with kids and also reading? Volunteer to read to the kids at a home for underprivileged youth. Or better yet, help them with their reading. Do you have a soft spot for the elderly and also love crafting? Volunteer at a senior living facility to lead a crafting class with easy-to-make projects. No matter what your interests are and which groups you'd like to give your time to, there's someone out there who needs you and will appreciate what you do. I'm a baker and I love to spend a cold winter Sunday at home whipping up all sorts of delectable concoctions. When I worked in an office it was easy to unload the fruits of my labor. I would bring my delicacies into the office on Monday mornings. You've never seen a group of people more thankful or more in need of a sugar rush to jumpstart their week. At one place I worked they even bought me a baker's apron with my name and "Pastry Chef" embroidered on it. When I started working from home several years ago, I all but stopped baking. I had no outlet for my confections and I certainly wasn't going to bake an entire cake or batch of cookies for myself. But I missed the baking and so I thought about what I could do. One of my neighbors is a firefighter and I asked him if his station would appreciate homemade baked goods once in a while. Duh! So, I started baking for the firefighters and have received so much gratitude and appreciation, but it's really me who's grateful for what they do on a daily basis and for how I can give back to them!

If you're really not the volunteering type and putting yourself out there to do good deeds for others on a regular basis is just not you, that's okay, it doesn't make you a bad person, it's just not your thing. Or maybe you just simply don't have the time. If you spend a lot of time working or caring for children or other family members or friends, maybe you're not looking for ways to connect with others through volunteerism. Yet you still want that sense of goodwill that giving back to your community brings. There's always money, honey.

IF YOU CAN'T GIVE YOUR TIME THEN YOU CAN GIVE OF YOURSELF FINANCIALLY.

Charitable organizations need money just as much as they need volunteer hours. Some workplaces even have matching programs where they'll match a certain percentage of what you donate to charity. This doesn't mean you have to donate thousands or even hundreds of dollars. Twenty-five dollars here, fifty dollars there, it all adds up. Find a charity or two with mission statements in which you believe and give 'em a little financial help. And of course you can write those donations off of your taxes and who couldn't use that? I find that giving some of my time and some of my money is a winning combination for me.

I'll close this chapter with a personal volunteerism story that will hopefully inspire you. Several years ago I volunteered for a cat shelter in my city and found it rewarding, but had to give it up due to time constraints that I was under at the time. I got out from under those constraints and for several years I would think about going back to volunteering there, but for some reason I never pulled the trigger. It's like most changes we want to make in our lives – we have the desire to change, but then struggle with the follow through. Finally, at the beginning of this year I made a New Year's resolution to go back. I decided that a regularly scheduled volunteer shift wasn't for me due to my work schedule, but that I was interested in special events. Every month they send out a listing of the regular monthly events as well as any special events for that month, and you can sign up for what interests you and what fits your schedule. I end up signing up for at least one event a month and it has been a wonderful addition to my life. In exchange for my time I've received the joy of knowing that I'm contributing to a cause in which I believe. I feel a sense of belonging to this organization. I feel a sense of purpose when I realize how much they depend on volunteers like me. I know I've helped them out of a jam when I've been the only one or one of the only ones to sign up for a particular event. I've met some wonderful fellow volunteers and gotten to know some of the shelter staff. Everyone is always so friendly and thankful, it's just a wonderful environment to be a part of. I even find myself coming home from an event and thinking about how we can do it better next year and how I can contribute to that.

When you're single there's often times the feeling that you don't belong anywhere. You don't belong to a specific someone, you don't belong to the couples club like "everyone else," and you sometimes feel like you don't even belong in society. Finding yourself a great volunteer gig can provide you with a strong sense of belonging and purpose, as well as providing an organization with something they so desperately need. Connecting with others and giving back to your community is a win-win situation.

THE WORK

1. What activities do you enjoy doing where you could connect with others? Classes? Sports leagues? Book cubs? Crafting groups?

2. What can you do for others in your neighborhood or at work?

3. What causes speak to you that you might like to get involved with?

4. Are there organizations in your local area for which you can volunteer and connect not only with a cause but with other people, too?

5. Are you able and would you enjoy donating money to a cause?

6. Write out the steps you need to take to get from point A (where you are now) to point B (where you want to be). This is your plan for getting your community involvement in order.

CHAPTER 20

GETTING OUT OF YOUR COMFORT ZONE AND SETTING GOALS

The purpose of this book is to show you amazing single girls just how amazingly happy and fulfilled your lives can be on your own. It's to show you how you can live your best life as a single girl, no relationship required. In order to do this you absolutely must change your thinking about being single, which we covered in Part 1. Then you must figure out who you are in this world on your own and who you want to be. This is what Part 2 has been about. In addition to changing your thoughts in Part 1 you've also been asked to change some of your actions. You've been asked to analyze the specific aspects of your life that are the most important and see how they're working for you. If they're not working, then you've been given suggestions on how to make them work. This entails changing some of what you do on a daily basis. It requires you to put yourself out there in new ways and try new things that may make you uncomfortable. It also requires you to do a lot of things on your own and that makes some of you really uncomfortable. This discomfort is natural, of course, but I want you to start looking at it in a different way. I *never* ask you to do this! (wink)

Think about this: When you do things with other people, your enjoyment of the activity is 50% about sharing it with the other person and 50% about the activity itself. This is not necessarily a bad thing, as a lot of times an activity can actually be enhanced by sharing it with someone else.

WHEN YOU DO THINGS ON YOUR OWN, HOWEVER, IT'S ALL ABOUT YOUR OWN PERSONAL EXPERIENCE OF THE ACTIVITY.

There are actually many activities that I enjoy doing on my own more than I enjoy doing them with someone else. For example, hiking. I've been hiking by myself for probably the last 25 years and so I'm used to it, but I also really enjoy doing it on my own. I've also hiked with other people and here are the differences. When I hike with other people, there's conversation, at least during the times that we're not huffing and puffing. Whenever there's conversation your mind is more focused on what's being said than it is on what's going on around you. All you have to do is get behind someone in their car who's on their cell phone to know this. So, by having a conversation on a hike with someone else, you may get the joy of the conversation, but you miss out on a lot of the joy of what's going on around you – birds chirping, a chipmunk scuttling through the underbrush, the breeze through the leaves, the site of a squirrel as it's about to drop a pinecone on your head. When you hike with someone else, you're also at the mercy of how far and how fast they want to go. If you're ready to do six miles at a three-mile per hour pace so that you can get to the top of that mountain and back to your car in two hours, and your friend's idea of a long hike is taking a shortcut through the woods to the nearest Starbucks, then your dream of taking a selfie while posing on a rock on top of the world is probably going to be dashed. So, it depends on what you're after. If you're looking for stimulating conversation and a leisurely pace then a hike with someone else is probably going to suit you. But if you're like me and you're looking to commune with nature while getting in a good workout, then you're probably going to enjoy hiking on your own much more. You can enjoy both, of course, just know that you're going to get different things out of each experience.

This goes for all other activities, as well. There are going to be plenty of activities that you'll do on your own that are going to feel uncomfortable at first, but will eventually be things that you look forward to doing on your own. In fact, the more you do things alone the more used to it you'll get and at some point you'll actually start to enjoy it more than being with someone else. I once went wine tasting on a trip to California with my then bf, Frog #38. It was my first time in Napa Valley and I was ready to taste my way from one end to the other. Now, Frog #38 wasn't much of wine drinker, and in fact wasn't much of a drinker at all, but he knew how excited I was and so he gladly came along for the ride. At the first winery he spent his time perusing the well-stocked gift shop while I did my sampling at the tasting bar. At the second one he actually joined in on a couple of the wines. At the third one he was visibly uncomfortable at the little table on the terrace where I was being served a flight of champagne. And by the fourth one I could tell he was completely over it. So, we left glorious Napa Valley after just four wineries and found our hotel instead.

The next time I went to Napa Valley I chose my companion more carefully and brought along my fellow oenophile friend, Janie. We descended upon the wineries from dawn till dusk, tasting everything in our path like a couple of hangry locusts. But Janie tends to spend a lot of time at each winery, chatting up the pourers, chatting up the fellow tasters, in fact chatting up anyone she sees. It's one of the characteristics of her personality that I enjoy the most, but maybe not when I'm trying to get to every winery on my list in a matter of a couple of days. Don't get me wrong, I do my fair share of chatting, but I keep my eye on my tasting goal at the same time. Still, my second experience in Napa was much better than my first and I had a great time with my friend.

On my third trip to La Napa, I decided to go it alone. Having never been wine tasting by myself before, it was certainly guaranteed to be an experience. I decided to go for only two days and taste at six wineries per day. I chose the wineries and then chose the order in which I would taste based on their geographic locations (I'm not type A at all). On the first day I made it to all six wineries on my list, with a break for lunch in the middle, where I discovered that my third winery for that day had a bevy of picnic supplies and several picnic tables under the trees next to the winery. I had a glorious picnic by myself and ended up chatting with a very nice couple at the table next to me who told me about another winery that wasn't on my list, but also wasn't to be missed. So, I added that one to the end of my day and it was fantastic. The next day I made it to all six of the wineries on my list and stopped at a cute little café for lunch that I had seen the day before. I did plenty of chatting and met plenty of great people, tasted and bought some amazing wine, ate at the places I wanted to eat, did the things I wanted to do, and arrived home feeling rejuvenated, if not a little hungover.

So, you're going to think that the moral of this very gripping wine tasting story is that going wine tasting on your own is so much better than going with someone else. Not true. While my wine tasting experience with Frog #38 was less-than-thrilling, my experience with my friend was truly enjoyable, as was my experience on my own. I had two experiences that were great, just in different ways. While my experience with Janie was full of conversation and laughter, and collaboration on what we were going to do, where we were going to eat, where we were going to stay, etc, my experience on my own was full of doing exactly what I wanted to do when I wanted to do it, eating where I wanted, staying where I wanted, and having personal conversations with the people I met.

THE ACTUAL MORAL OF THIS STORY IS THAT YOU CAN HAVE JUST AS GOOD OF A TIME DOING SOMETHING YOU ENJOY ON YOUR OWN AS YOU CAN DOING IT WITH SOMEONE ELSE, AND MAYBE EVEN BETTER DEPENDING ON THE CIRCUMSTANCES.

It's also possible to spend birthdays and holidays alone and have a great time on your own, too. I usually get together with my family

244 Single Girl Bliss • Leslie Kaz

for Christmas, but every few years geography and circumstances make it better for us to spend the holiday at our separate residences, which of course for me means spending it alone or at least spending it with friends. While I enjoy Christmas with my family immensely, I have also found ways to enjoy it alone. There was the year that my friend, Tom, threw together an impromptu Christmas Eve dinner at his house for all the "orphans," and everyone brought their favorite dish. I made the most amazing mashed potatoes that year, and the setting was so intimate and the company so enjoyable that we all had a fantastic time.

Then there was the Christmas that I decided to spend completely alone, just to see what the experience would be like. I ended up having a wonderful time. I did all the things that I enjoy doing on my own at Christmastime. Sleeping in, then getting Dunkin' Donuts for "brunch" on Christmas Eve morning. Watching my fave Christmas cartoons all day then going for a walk down to the lake in the afternoon. Apps and champagne for dinner, with a viewing of "A Christmas Carol" before bed. On Christmas Day, gifts in the morning, including watching the cats get silly on their new catnip toys that Santa left in their stocking. Phone calls to family, music all day, a favorite movie in the afternoon followed by a luxurious bubble bath, a dinner of steak and lobster, and more champagne. Christmas tree lights twinkling, a happy cat on either side of me, candles glowing, champagne in hand (are we sensing a theme here?). Do married people ever get the chance to just sit and focus on the beauty of something (like my lit up Christmas village on a snowy evening) and daydream? While I thoroughly enjoy spending Christmas with my family, for three days anyway, I wouldn't trade that Christmas entirely alone for anything.

I've also spent birthdays by myself. Last year I took myself out for lunch to one of my fave restaurants, then hit the bundt cake shop for a special b-day dessert, then to the mall for some shopping, then to the spa for a pedi, and finally ended up meeting friends for happy hour. When they asked how I spent my birthday and I told them, they all agreed that was the perfect way to spend the day. And you know, it was. Instead of hoping for those events to take place and then relying on someone else to make them happen, with the potential for great disappointment, I just made them happen for myself and everything went exactly as I'd wanted. I've spent several birthdays on my own in the manner described above and I've never been disappointed. Now, I've also spent many a birthday with friends and significant others that have been great, too, but the point I'm trying to make is that you can spend these occasions by yourself, as well, and they can turn out just as good, if not better, than when you depend on someone else to make your day special for you. If spending Christmas or Thanksgiving or your birthday alone sounds like something you could never do or would never even want to try, those are just your thoughts about what it could be like. It could also be the best thing you've ever done for yourself. If you think it's going to be terrible it probably will be. On the other hand, if you think it could be great and plan it out so that you set yourself up for success, then it probably will be great. Letting your fear of doing something you've never done before keep you from experiencing something that could be wonderful is the surest way to not live your best life.

I went through this a bit when I started my own biz and went from working in an office with hundreds of other people around to working by myself at home. So, now, not only was I single and childless, I also didn't have coworkers anymore. Talk about feeling

ALONE! For years I worked in busy offices, surrounded by people all day every day, so my "lonely" nights and weekends were actually a welcome respite from that. Being alone all day every day should've been painful, right? Not gonna lie, it was difficult at first. I didn't miss a whole lot about working in an office, but I did miss the office comradery. In the long run, though, working from home didn't make me lonelier, it actually did the opposite. I learned how to enjoy being alone every day.

THAT'S WHAT EVERYTHING YOU DO THAT YOU'VE NEVER DONE BEFORE IS, A LEARNING EXPERIENCE.

Some learning experiences are not going to be good ones for you and you're going to have to decide that that particular activity cannot be done by you on your own. Like maybe you try traveling by yourself and you're either so nervous or scared or bored that you just don't enjoy it at all. That's okay, you don't have to enjoy doing everything by yourself and thankfully you'll have friends, family and a wide social circle to get you around that. But there are going to be things that you find you enjoy just as much, if not more, on your own. Give things a chance, give them some time, and you'll set yourself free.

I think it's important to talk about goal-setting at this point. You're about to embark on a journey of self-discovery and life-changing choices, all in a good way that's going to get you to your best life, but it's going to be difficult to get there if you don't set some goals for yourself. Goal setting starts with knowing your "why." You may have heard this statement before, as figuring out your "why" is a big topic in the self-development community these days. Finding your why means determining the big reason that you want to get from point A to point B. For the single girl who wants to take her life down a new path, your why might be something like wanting to stop wasting your life and start living your best life now, regardless of relationship status. Or your why might be to give up the relentless Endless Search and start focusing on your best life. Or your why might simply be just to be happy. Regardless of what your why is, it's important to define it so that you understand why you're doing this for yourself.

THE ROAD IS GOING TO BE BUMPY ALONG THE WAY AND KEEPING YOUR WHY IN MIND IS WHAT'S GOING TO GET YOU THROUGH.

My why for wanting to start my own biz was to be my own boss, call my own shots, and be responsible for my own financial success. Those things were far more important to me than the struggles I went through in building a business. What's your why for wanting to start a new journey in your life?

And what's your path for getting there? What are your goals? A good place to start is with the exercise in chapter 13 where you defined where you are now and where you'd like to be. Now rewrite your story. Write your story as you see yourself now and then how you'll be five years from now. Come at it from a feeling of confidence and happiness. Instead of writing, "I've been miserably single for

10 years," how about, "I've been on the adventurous journey of dating for 10 years. It's had its ups and downs, but it's also been an experience of learning and self-discovery. Now I'm embarking on a new journey that's all about me and it's going to be the best one yet." Proceed with where you want to get to. What are you doing for a job? How much money do you make? Where do you live? What kinds of friends do you have and what do you do together? How healthy and fit are you? What kinds of activities do you engage in on a daily/weekly/monthly basis? Are you a skydiving, Mandarin-speaking, certified sommelier? How do you give back to your community? You're probably leading skydiving expeditions in China where you lead them through a wine tasting afterward. Whatever your new story is, addressing it from where you are now and where you'd like to be is going to frame up your goals for you. Look at the progression and figure out what steps you need to take to get from point A (where you are now) to point B (where you'll be in five years). Assign some due dates to each step within each of your goals and embark on your exciting new journey to living your best life.

Remember, you're venturing into the unknown and that can be scary. There are going to be times when you're going to want to quit. There are going to be times when you're going to want to go back to living your unhappy, but comfortable, life. There are going to be times when you're going to think you can't do this. What person who's ever achieved anything great has not gone through these same emotions? You've heard the expression, "Nothing worth having is ever easy to get?" It's because it's true! Do you think an Olympic gymnast LOVES every minute of every grueling workout and it all just comes easily to her? You think she LOVES falling on her back while dismounting the uneven parallel bars, LOVES hitting her head on the balance beam when she slips during a back flip, and LOVES landing on her ass after a botched vault? Hells no! It's hard! Freaking hard! But she does it because she wants something bigger than what all those missteps add up to. She wants to be the best. If she can do a round-off, double back handspring, back tuck with a full twist, and stick her landing, you can certainly sign up for a class in something new!

THE WORK

1. What things have you never done on your own that you could definitely see yourself doing alone?

2. What things have you never done on your own that you're scared to do on your own, but can see giving it a try?

3. What things have you never done, period, and you're looking forward to trying, whether on your own or not?

4. What goals can you set for yourself in the future? What is your "why" for each of these goals?

5. What is your current story? Write it out. My name is... I live in... I work at... and so on.

6. Now rewrite your story the way you'd like it to read instead.

7. Write out the steps you need to take to get from point A (where you are now) to point B (where you want to be). This is your plan for getting your goals in order.

CHAPTER 21

SINGLE GIRL BLISS!

Here we are at the final chapter of this book. This whole book has been about changing your thoughts about being single so that you see your singleness as something positive rather than something negative. It's also been about giving up The Endless Search, at least temporarily, so that you can focus on creating your best life or yourself right now. And finally it's been about defining who you are and who you want to be. You now have a plan to get from where you are to where you want to be and you're excited as hell about it! So, basically this book has been about celebrating your singleness and making it something to be happy about, not something you don't want and are stuck with. In this final chapter I'm going to leave you with all of the ways the single life is oh-so-blissful.

THE NUMBER ONE GREAT THING ABOUT BEING SINGLE IS YOUR PERSONAL FREEDOM.

This is something single people have that no other group can quite measure up to. Especially if you're single with no kids or your kids are grown and on their own. You get to do what you want, when you want, and how you want to do it. Now, this doesn't mean that you have ultimate freedom. You still have the constraints of money, work and other commitments, but as long as you have the money and the time, you can be out there conquering the world. You don't have to worry about what the person in your life wants to do, what they want to spend money on, where they want to go, etc. You get to just do. And since this is the one area where couples really envy their single friends, why not rub it in their faces as much as possible? Ha! I have a friend who loves to subtly bring up the fact that I'm single and she's in a relationship every time we're together. I guess she thinks this is something she has over me? So, I make sure to tell her about all the great solo travel I do, events I go to, and activities I participate in that she'll never get to do because her husband isn't amenable to those things. Take that!

Even the little personal freedoms that you have add up. My dad likes music and my mom isn't a big fan, so he doesn't get to play music around the house. He particularly likes jazz and she particularly doesn't, so jazz is out of the question even on the car radio. Even when he's home alone it doesn't even occur to him to play music because he's spent the past 50 years not playing it. Is playing music better than having a loving partner? No, of course not. But if he didn't have her it would be a way to enjoy his life fully. When you're in a relationship, you have that relationship and hopefully you're happy with it, even with all of its constraints.

WHEN YOU'RE SINGLE, THERE ARE NO CONSTRAINTS UNLESS THEY'RE SELF-IMPOSED, SO YOU GET TO HAVE ALL OF THE THINGS THAT YOU WANT INSTEAD.

Is one better than the other? Maybe, maybe not. The point is that when you're single you may not have a partner, but you have other things instead. Other things that couples don't have. It's like you're in a relationship with yourself and you like to do all of the same things that you like to do, eat all of the same things that you like to eat, go all of the same places that you want to go, spend money on all of the same things that you like to spend money on, and listen to jazz in the house if you want to.

There are also myriad opportunities out there that are available to single people that are less available to couples. Singles believe that they live in a couples' world and in many ways we do, but we have our own advantages, as well. If your job offers you a transfer to the Australia office, how much easier is it going to be to accept that offer if you're single? If for whatever reason your partner couldn't or wouldn't go, you'd really have to miss out on the opportunity to live in Australia. Or what about something simpler like clubs or activities that are just for singles? I don't believe there are any clubs that are just for married people even if most of them seem to be. Even timeshare invitations have changed. It used to be that you had to be married or at least cohabitating in order to get in on those cheapo vacation offers where they make you sit through their painful timeshare spiel as penance. I recently got an invitation to one in Maui that said you had to be either married, cohabitating, or in a "life partnership" to be eligible. I consider myself to be in a "life partnership" with all of my close friends, so I think I'll invite one of them. Hopefully they'll forgive me for subjecting them to the timeshare salespeople when they see the pool!

There's also the freedom to do things at the drop of a hat and not have to consider anyone else in your decision making. I once had a weekend trip planned to Chicago with a friend. When that friend was unable to go at the last minute, I asked another friend who was single and she just said yes without even thinking twice about it. That same friend is married today and I can guarantee she'd have to check with her husband, check their schedule, and check their bank account first. On the flip side, I had a friend tell me that she had a weekend trip planned to wine country in Oregon and that the friend she was going with dropped out at the last minute so she was going by herself. Without missing a beat I said, "I'll go!" If I want to join something, I join it. If I want to quit something, I quit it. If I want to go somewhere, I go. There's no asking permission or checking with someone or considering feelings. You just do what you want to do. If you think this is no big advantage, ask a married friend, especially one with kids, what's the biggest thing she misses about being single.

OWN YOUR FREEDOM, SINGLE GIRL, AND FLAUNT THE HELL OUT OF IT!

Single people tend to think that their lives are uncertain because they're on their own. What if this happens or what if that happens? I'll have no one to lean on when it does and no one to help me make it go away. In fact, your life is more certain when you're single because you never have to wonder what that other person's actions are going to mean for you. When you're part of a couple, the what if this happens and what if that happens is doubled because there are two people. What if he loses his job, can't/won't find another, and you have to support him? What if he cheats on you and walks out on your marriage after 25 years? What if he gets caught committing insider trading and goes to jail? What are you going to tell Grandma then? When you're on your own you have only you to worry about. And since you have complete control over your own actions, you make sure you don't get caught up in insider trading and everything will be alright.

Imagine spending your whole life married to someone and then getting to the end and wondering if you made the right choice. Wondering if you could've had a whole different, and better, life. We've all had instances like this. What if I had taken this job instead of that one, where would I be now? What if I had moved to that city instead of this one, what would my life be like now? What if I had bought Microsoft stock in the '80's instead of going on that blackjack spree in Vegas? As a blissful single girl you won't ever have to wonder whether you married the wrong Frog and spent your entire life with him. You're spending your entire life with YOU and even though you'll still have to lament that missed stock purchase opportunity, you won't ever have to wonder whether you gave the power over your life and its happiness to someone else.

YOU HAVE THE OPPORTUNITY TO INSTEAD LOOK BACK ON YOUR LIFE AND LOVE EVERY MINUTE OF IT.

We've all played the oh-poor-me single girl at one time or another. "Why can't I find someone?" "What's wrong with me?" "Why can't I just be happy like you guys," you say to your married friends. I think I've shown that the grass is most definitely not always greener on the other side, but we've all played this victim role at some point. Our married friends have consoled us and taken pity on us, and promised to introduce us to their cousin George once he gets through his terrible divorce and off anti-depressants. But even while our married friends are pitying us, a part of them is secretly hoping that we stay single because deep down they know how good we have it even if we don't. Once you get your life together your married friends will no longer pity you, they'll envy you! They won't have poor sad-sack you to deal with anymore, they'll have amazing, blissful single-girl you. You're that girl who has it all together – great job, great home, loads of friends, always on the go, climbing mountains, always giving back. Oh, and you speak French, too! They'll look at their own lives and wonder what they've been doing now that you've created all of this for yourself, by yourself. Washing someone else's dirty socks? Suddenly you're the one doing the consoling and the pitying, and trying to encourage them to take their lives in a new direction. Now you're way too good for lame cousin George and they know it!

I meet new people all the time and some of the first questions they ask are: Are you married? Do you have kids? Sometimes I answer, "No, I chose happiness." It's meant as a joke and they take it as such and laugh. But then they look at me with a nod of their heads and a knowing expression on their faces, and I know they get what I'm talking about. That even the greatest of relationships and the most awesome of kids come with their downfalls. Their maintenance, their annoyances, their trials and tribulations, their downright heartaches. By choosing to forgo all of that, I've chosen a different level of happiness. Not better, necessarily, just far less dependent on others.

You will know that you've achieved true happiness as a single person when you're experiencing a moment that would normally be shared with someone else and it feels perfect exactly as it is. There's a story in the book "Chicken Soup for the Single's Soul," that's written by a man, Bryan Aubrey. After spending years and years in his own Endless Search, he has an epiphany that changes his life forever. He writes, "One morning a few years ago, I had just returned home from the gym, which I had found to be an interesting, if so far unproductive, place to scout for Soulmate-in-Skimpy-Workout-Gear. It was spring and the lilacs in my yard were in bloom. I sat on the deck with a Styrofoam cup of coffee in my hand, looking out on the display of nature's greenery. It wasn't the high from the workout or the coffee that did it, but I gradually became aware that everything in that moment was perfect. Everything was exactly as it should be. Nothing else was needed. Nothing added or subtracted from that minute could possibly "improve" it. This certainly wasn't the way I normally felt, having conditioned myself to believe that what every minute really needed was a quick infusion of Soulmate. And yet that moment shifted something inside me. I don't know how or why, but I do know that it has continued, that there is a tranquil "place" inside me, that is no place at all, because it is everywhere and nowhere, and it is still and silent and has neither beginning nor end and is not alien or foreign to me or outside of me. After years of searching, I have found my soulmate, and it is myself. The bachelor is content."

LET ME SHARE WITH YOU
MY OWN PERSONAL JOURNEY TO SINGLE GIRL BLISS.

After deciding to give up The Endless Search and get control of my own life and happiness, the following things happened: I left my 20-year foray in the corporate world to start my own business and be my own boss. I now run two successful businesses and I'm more fulfilled with the work I do than I ever could've dreamed possible. I finally had the time to get my home in shape and I now love where I live. My home is my sanctuary, it's beautiful, and it reflects my personality and the way I live. I've met so many new people in starting and running my businesses that my friend circle is now so wide I can hardly keep up with it. I'm grateful for my friends, new and long-time, every single day, and they bring light and happiness to my life. I've also started focusing more on my relationship with my parents. I realize they won't be around forever and I want to make sure I don't have any regrets where they're concerned when they're gone. I've forgiven and forgotten, and realized that all people are flawed and are basically doing the best that they can. I've changed my diet and started an exercise routine that are quickly getting me to a place of good health and fitness, without feeling deprived or exhausted. I've come to realize that it's about your health, not what size you wear or how you look in a bikini. I've made a bucket list of personal things I want to accomplish – places I want to go, things I want to try, books I want to read, languages I want to speak – and I'm working through my list as you read this book. I've started volunteering with an animal welfare organization and I feel great every time I do something for them. I've met a lot of great people while volunteering, too, and they've only enhanced my experience of life. Basically, I've created the life I've always wanted, minus a relationship, and I take so much pride and joy that I've managed to do this on my own. In case you're sitting there thinking that this all sounds great, but it's something you could never do, remember that I was once exactly where you are now and I got myself to where I am now by applying the principles in this book. It wasn't easy. It didn't happen overnight. I had to put in the mindset work as well as making actual changes in my life. My brain fought me the whole way and there were obstacles to overcome. But I did it. You can do it, too, single girl. You can find your bliss.

ACKNOWLEDGMENTS

Thank you to all the men (aka frogs) I ever dated and the one I married. If it had worked out with any one of you, this book would not have happened.

Thank you to my parents, who are pretty conservative and don't always understand my "wild hairs," but who supported the writing of this book and the development of my business, LESLIEKAZ.COM.

Also thank you to Natalie McGuire of Natalie McGuire Designs, who designed the fabulous cover of this book and formatted the entire thing.

Finally, special thanks to all the single girls in my life for navigating the ups and downs with me over the years and providing stories for me to share, and to all of my other friends, as well, without whom I wouldn't be journeying through this single-girl life nearly as blissfully.

.

ABOUT THE AUTHOR

Leslie Kaz is a confirmed single girl dedicated to helping other single women find their bliss. She is an author, speaker and certified life coach, who has helped numerous single women transform their lives. Leslie is living happily ever after with her two cats, Flop and Murphy.

YOU CAN LEARN MORE ABOUT LESLIE AND GET ON HER MAILING LIST BY VISITING LESLIEKAZ.COM.

TO DELVE DEEPER INTO THE TOPICS
COVERED IN THIS BOOK OR IF YOU NEED
HELP IMPLEMENTING THEM INTO YOUR LIFE,

I OFFER COACHING PROGRAMS THAT GET YOU FROM WHERE YOU ARE TO WHERE YOU WANT TO BE.

We go in-depth into your thinking, beliefs and mindset to find out what's holding you back from happiness. We also explore who you really are and who you'd like to be. We create an action plan for your life so that you can begin to live your happiest, best life right now.

VISIT LESLIEKAZ.COM TO LEARN MORE
AND SEE ADDITIONAL PRODUCTS AND INFORMATION.

CHAPTER 5

AWFUL, UNTRUE, LIMITING THOUGHT #4 "I NEED TO BE TAKEN CARE OF"

L adies, this is not the 1950's. You are not June Cleaver vacuuming the living room in a dress, heels and pearls, just waiting for your man to come home so that your life can be complete. Maybe back then women needed to be taken care of by men, although World War II and Rosie the Riveter kind of shot that theory all to hell. Even so, after the war things pretty much went back to the way they were for another fifteen years or so. But nowadays women can do anything for themselves that a man can do for them, except for a few heavy lifting-type situations for which you'll need a burly friend or neighbor.

Do you need a man's paycheck or are you rockin' the career thing all on your own? If you're not making what you'd like to and you think it would be so much easier to just have a man take care of that part, well sure, it would be so much easier, but is that your reality right now? Do you truly NEED a man to provide you with more money? Is there absolutely no way you could make that money for yourself? Or is it just that you haven't considered the ways, hoping that Mr-Right-with-Fat-Paycheck will come strolling into your life in the produce aisle? If money is your issue, and believe me I know whereof I preach, there are ways to get it that don't involve The Endless Search. Or prostitution. For one thing, you're likely not making the same amount as your male counterparts, so the first thing you should do is ask for a raise at work.

My personal story around "I need a man for financial support" thinking arose when I decided to change careers. I was drowning in a 20-year career full of drab-grey cubicles, mind-numbing work and soul-crushing meetings, working for companies who claimed to care about their employees. Thankfully I knew what I wanted to do instead and I went back to night school to get another degree in interior design. My dream was to start my own residential interior design business. And all I needed was a husband to support me while I did it. When I graduated with my degree, I still had no husband, had gotten laid off from my job, and instead of listening to what the Universe was trying to tell me, I got another soul-crushing job just like my last one. But one thing was different. When I started that job I said to myself, "I'm only going to be here 2-5 years and then I'm starting my design business." Sure enough, less than three years later I was out on my own with my new business. I used the time that I was at that company to save up a little cushion, and as fate would have it, there was a round of layoffs right when I was planning my exit strategy. So, not only did I have the money I'd saved, but I also made it out of there with a nice severance package to boot. I'm not going to say that those first few years weren't a struggle financially, the anxiety about it all almost did me in, but then it got easier and led to bigger and better things, and I didn't need a husband to support me after all, just the Universe.